D1692628

Cody

Life Lessons

Inspired by My Spirited Mare

The authentic experiences

of Reneé Budde

Follow Cody on Facebook@
CodyBookLifeLessons

Listen to CODY
Life Lessons by My Spirited Mare
on Audible.com

e-books available on:
Amazon.com

Published by Sojourn Publishing
Third Edition
© 2021 by Reneé Budde All rights reserved.

Library of Congress Registration
Number
TX000747 6784 2011-15-15

ISBN
#978-0-9846635-5-2

**Where thrill and faith collide!
Horse enthusiast or not,
Cody's not just a horse ride,
it's a pearl dive!**

GLOSSARY OF EQUINE TERMS

General terms

Broodmare: a female horse (mare) used solely for reproducing

Gelding: male horse, whose reproductive hardware has been altered

Green broke: A horse with minimal training

Greenhorn: a person lacking experience or knowledge

Herd: a group of animals that roam together

Mare: female horse, which on occasion, can be temperamental

Quarter Horse: the fastest horse bred to run one quarter of a mile

Anatomy of a Horse

Fetlocks: the feather-like hair above the back of the hooves

Forelock: lock of hair on the forehead

Frog: tough flexible V-shaped pad under a horse's hoof

Hindquarters or haunches: rear of the horse

Hock: joint in the hind leg

Hoof: foot of a horse

Mane: the hair on the top of an animal's neck

Tack Terms

Cinch or Girth: the under strap of a saddle, used to anchor the saddle on the horse

Headstall: headpiece with a ring on the bottom to which a lead rope can be attached

Lead rope: a rope used to lead a horse

Pony: to lead a horse with a rope from the back of another horse

Reins: straps used at the head in conjunction with a bit in the mouth to control and direct the horse

Saddle: a seat on the animal, which holds the rider

Saddle horn: the projection like a horn at the arch of the front of a Western saddle

Stirrup: rider's foot support hanging down from each side of the saddle

Trailering: to be transported by a trailer

Whip: a long, flexible, slim tool used to train (not a tool for beating); there is no rope attached to the end as one might think.

ACKNOWLEDGEMENTS:

First and foremost, to my daughter Sunshine Thomas, aka Little Bird. Sunshine is responsible for the front cover lay out and photography.

To Mr. Budde, for the vision, encouragement and tech skills you brought to the table to make this endeavor possible. Thank you for believing in me. Your insightful humor makes me laugh and stretches me beyond myself. You are brilliant as well as extraordinarily good-looking!

My sister Denise Karnes helped in the beginning stages of the book, she verified my recall of the stories and reminded me of pieces forgotten. Thank you, Denise.

Diana Stuhlmann, thank you for your fitly spoken words, "Don't limit the book, it could be exceedingly, abundantly above whatever you would think, ask or even imagine possible." Your insightfulness pushed me to think beyond a coffee table book. Without your encouraging words, I would never have thought "Cody" possible. Thank you.

To Leigh Ann Tuttle for enduring my laughter at you when you made the outrageous suggestion, make it a series, Cody and Friends, Cody Goes to Washington, Cody Learns to Drive. Who would have thought?

An enormous thank you to my behind-the-scene team of editors and proofreaders:

The biggest heartfelt credit goes to Melissa Young, who transformed scribbled notes into a book worth reading.

Lisa, my dear friend, THANK YOU does not begin to express my gratitude for your steadfast diligence in the monumental task of stretching me beyond. I cannot overstate my appreciation of your labor of love for the instructional edit and proof of the latest Cody edition. I apologize in advance, when my creative independence overrules your skill and highly sought-after recommendations.

Deb Hommas and Rowena Marris, thank you for being willing participants in the proof-reading process. Your sacrificial donation to the cause cannot be overstated.

Interior photography by Sunshine Thomas, Tonya Vander and Reneé Budde.

Dedicated to all the Dream Wranglers,

who have vision and courage

to step outside the box

and be refreshingly different.

I dedicate this book to you.

TABLE OF CONTENTS:

Chapter 1	Ruined	page 12
Chapter 2	Release	page 16
Chapter 3	Plunge	page 22
Chapter 4	Ride, Baby, Ride	page 30
Chapter 5	Pigheaded	page 36
Chapter 6	In the Saddle	page 46
Chapter 7	Cody Takes Flight	page 54
Chapter 8	Grooming	page 68
Chapter 9	Misty	page 76
Chapter 10	Floozy	page 86
Chapter 11	Broken Heart	page 94
Chapter 12	Home on the Range	page 98
Chapter 13	Big Move	page 104
Chapter 14	Protection	page 114
Chapter 15	Friends	page 126
Chapter 16	Trailering	page 136
Chapter 17	Hall Ranch	page 148
Chapter 18	Crossing the Platte	page 154
Chapter 19	The Park	page 166
Chapter 20	Road Blocks	page 178
Chapter 21	Goodbye	page 186
Chapter 22	Buddy	page 192
Chapter 23	Ralston Creek	page 204
Chapter 24	Mother's Day	page 210
Chapter 25	Strangers	page 216
Chapter 26	Choose Life	page 224
Chapter 27	Time Heals	page 238

Priceless excerpt   page 254

Oil portrait of Cody by Joan Ames

RB

Ruined

1

There are occurrences in our lives that are fleeting. Others linger and become a part of our very core. Unlike garment foundations that mask and rearrange what lies beneath, true foundations require time. They impact our lives, change them forever. The stories you are about to encounter are those foundations for me. My name is Reneé. I've been told I have a unique perspective. As these pages unfold, you will experience with me the lessons that revolutionized my life. Hold on for the ride!

Life is full of opportunities, choices and pearls.

Treasures don't lie in plain sight;

they hide below the surface.

Embrace the hunt, dive in.

Hear tell, horses and boats have one thing in common: they are a hole into which you throw money. OK, so horses cost money, but so do dogs, cats, hobbies, motorcycles, and cars. Pretty much anything connected to fun costs money.

Life looked different after the week we spent at a low budget dude ranch in Cody, Wyoming. You know, when you look back and say, "That experience changed my life;" it was one of those vacations. At the time it was just another vacation in an old log cabin with bunk beds, a step above camping. A handful of handsome wranglers work the ranch. These fellas are everything from the entertainment, to housekeepers and cooks. Multi-talented, competent, and skilled, wranglers they are! A great catch for any gal (who happens to be old enough to marry, that is).

My eleven-year-old, who looks fifteen, is a cute addition to the crowded barn with her chocolate curls flirting about. Sunshine's distinctive almond eyes keep watch on young wranglers asserting authority. Mares and geldings willingly oblige their hooves. Dirt and manure hurl through the air as wranglers in tight jeans pick horse hooves clean. Sunshine and I are mesmerized.

Turning my nose up, I inquire, "Doesn't that smell bother you?"

Slowly the rugged cowhand answers, "Well, ma'am, it's better than the perfume those women wear in the bars."

Enough said.

Our young, handsome, blond guide, Les, wears a silver oversized belt buckle and a wide black felt hat as big as himself, accentuating his tall lean body. Les is taking a special interest in caring for us. Not sure if he's working the tip angle or wooing Sunshine. Possibly, he's fond of her mama. I guess another possibility is that Les is genuinely a nice guy. I have my suspicions.

Les, an interesting cowboy with great stories, opens up as we trail ride through the Wyoming hills, "My sister rides bulls in the rodeo."

"Bulls? Why bulls?" I quiz.

"She's afraid of horses."

Here we are, a couple of greenhorns, on the back of a horse and he tells us his sister's fear of horses! His story is slightly unsettling. What is he thinkin'?!

"Why?"

"She says a bull wants to kill you, this she knows. A horse, on the other hand, can be just as dangerous. You can't trust a horse. They'll sneak up on you unawares and kill you! So, she opts to ride bulls."

"That's just crazy." Sunshine expresses my sentiments exactly.

"Do you people like rodeo?"

Sunshine and I don't know how to answer that. We've never seen one. With a shrug of the shoulders in unison, and harmonize, "I don't know."

"There's one in town, you ought to go. It's a lot of fun. My sister rides bulls on Saturday night."

I mention to Les, "We might look into buying a horse for Sunshine. She loves animals." Now we have never discussed owning a horse; those words just flew out of my mouth with the greatest of ease. Casual conversation tossed to the side, Les begins to impart his equine expertise on horse procurement. "A mature horse is what Sunshine needs. Oh, say, ten to fifteen years old. Purchase either a well-mannered gelding or mare. Mares are moodier than their counterparts." Eyeing my daughter with pleasure, he continues, "You don't want to wrestle with a stud; they're too much for a kid to handle." With a quick glance over his shoulder, we connect eyes.

"Noted."

With his expertise, Les pours out great advice to our attentive ears.

"Choose a healthy animal, of course. Don't buy a sick one. Make certain it's surefooted, not easily tripped or gimped up. Pay no mind to its color; some of the prettiest are the stupidest."

We circle back toward the stable; Les gives us the OK to run the horses. Scared out of our wits, bouncing hinnies fly! What power, strength and alleged control!

After an hour wrestling a stiff saddle we drop to the ground. Bow-legged and barely able to walk, we emerge with great enthusiasm about ownership possibilities. The young wrangler gently nods with a slight tip of his hat in recognition of our gratitude.

"That should get you started."

I might be delirious, but I have the distinct impression the wranglers spent more time with us than any of the other guests.

We left the ranch chock-full of ideas. Those wranglers plumb ruined us.

RB

Release

2

Six weeks later, we enter the unknown, the world of equine. Not sure how this all happened, but we find ourselves hooked up with Westernaires. This youth precision-drill team has been around since the beginning of time. We are impressed with this all-volunteer well-oiled machine.

Instill confidence within an adolescent.

Then add responsibility.

Children can be taught any skill.

Sunshine takes to Westernaires like flies on manure. Today is our first evening in Tenderfoot class. You don't need to be a horse owner to join. I speculate this barn is filled with novice urbanites just like us. A horse is provided by the organization for each child. Enthusiasm and chatter fill the chilly indoor arena. Parents' butts snuggle close together to warm the metal bleachers, as they introduce themselves, pointing out their children. Some men huddle together, while others isolate themselves on the sideline.

Really cool dads shiver against the cement back wall with shoulders slouched inward. Cold hands are jammed into pockets unless your hand is wrapped snuggly around a mug. Oh look, over there, against the wall, you'll find Sunshine's papa. He's the one with the gray, curly ponytail that pokes out under his ball cap. Do you see him? He's still nursing this morning's coffee. You'll never see him without a mug in hand. For the most part, Ben is a quiet sort. He suffers tonight because smoking is not allowed on the floor.

Me? Well, I sit by myself on the bleachers. It's tough being a married single. The air is thick with tension. Germs are camouflaged as dust particles. Fifty or more horses line up waiting for their little counterparts to tend to their grooming needs. Those of us with nothing better to do are annoyed by the mere presence of the fly brigade. Tails swish to torture the little buzzards. A horse tail violently swings with intent towards my daughter's face.

I cringe as the battle unfolds, conversatin' with myself:

"Yikes!"

"Watch out, Little Bird!"

"OUCH! That must hurt!"

"Nasty flies. They are such a nuisance, aren't they?"

The wrangler's voice is heard faintly in the background. Annoying fly infiltration has derailed my attention.

"Listen up, kids! Horses communicate by ESP. Pay attention to their voice; horses will let you know what they think."

The students move on, but I dangle in the twilight zone. The notion horses communicate with ESP! "What a ridiculous statement." In disbelief I mutter, "Oh, sure they do. Huh! What an outrageous idea!"

I fix my eyes and gasp for air as Sunshine effortlessly slides under the belly of an intimidating, giant equine specimen. My daughter crosses from beneath the horse with comfort and ease. Granted, she is limber and not the size of an adult. Still, just her bravery makes me cringe. As if that wasn't enough, she walks right behind the horse! I'm telling you, she is touching him! Look, she rubs her hand across the horse's rump as she passes.

Isn't this dangerous? Sunshine, you might get kicked! Sitting on the edge of my seat, gnawing at my cuticles, I can scarcely watch. As if engaged in a thriller movie, panic-stricken, I wonder what will happen next!

If that's not bad enough, the kids pick up the animals' legs and brace them one at a time on their own legs. A skinny little tool resembling a hook is used by small children to pick buried manure from giant hooves. Those hooves are the size of my hand, or bigger. How do these kids do that?

"Phew! Does that ever smell foul!"

My nose curls, my face distorts with disgust. The stench drastically changes the air quality. Hear tell some people find this fragrance enjoyable.

The head wrangler dude barks instructions, "Work the pick away from the horse, not toward him. You don't want to injure you or the frog (the V shape in the hoof). Dig deep to get all the manure."

Restless in my seat, jittering about, totally intimidated by the size of these giant creatures. On one hand, it's terribly exciting, on the other, horribly frightening. My mind joins the battle zone of conflict. As a mother, I want to protect my child. Why would I put her in harm's way? Why would I intentionally do that? Life is full enough of unavoidable mishaps.

I cannot protect my daughter from everything.

After all, I'm not God.

Release her

to make decisions and mistakes on her own.

That is how kids learn.

Right?

Questions clutter my mind with disturbing scenarios. Fear on the rampage. Reality kicks in! What if she's injured? Permanently scarred for life? Killed? These things happen, you know. The list is endless. Sunshine is my only child and there will be no more.

Consciously muttering over and over to myself, "Reneé, let it go. You will never protect her from all life's dangers."

I must make a conscious decision.

Quit holding on so tight to my precious child.

She must grow up sometime.

Let go of apprehension.

Choose to embrace the experience

for what it is.

Trust the Lord with her protection.

Give it a chance. I just might like it.

It's Saturday, the day masses of children gather for an hour-long ride. Sunshine chooses a large, dappled-gray equine specimen. Smokey is a rickety, thirty-year-old horse; most don't live to be as old and cantankerous as he. Midway through the ride, Smokey lowers his head and lifts his hindquarters upward! Well, if that isn't an attempt to buck off a young rider, I don't know what is! Sunshine holds her own, not allowing him to get the best of her! She remains in the saddle and gets Smokey under control. My eleven-year-old, controlling this ole buckin' horse, NO WAY! Not only was she NOT afraid or intimidated, but she wore an infectious smile as big as the sky! I didn't see it, but I heard all about it from her instructor. The news traveled like wildfire! My daughter, the talk of the stable!

My heart swells with pride as I grow an inch or two taller. My chest extends outward, my nose breathes more clearly in higher elevation. This smug face of mine, being the animated type, shows everything, including the biggest, proudest grin a parent can possibly express, unashamed, hidden from no one.

This is my daughter! Color me surprised! I can't help but admire Sunshine's natural aptitude with horses. She's not intimidated by size or danger.

You go, girl!

RB

Plunge

3

Sunshine's confidence and ability vastly improve. Mom's fears subside. The decision to take the plunge is made. There's wind of a horse for sale within the Westernaires family.

The confident, slender blonde, surrounded by a swarm of intrigued parents, is Sherrie. "Cody is fourteen years old and a little goofy. She requires a more confident rider," Sherry aggressively pitches her bay as the crowd enlarges. ("Bay" is the term used for the mare's coloring and marking.) "I've been training her the past four years. She has great ground manners, takes the lead with a herd. By herself, she's a little skittish and fearful." Apologetically, Sherrie continues, "Cody does best with a companion."

Without any thought given, words freely fly right out of my mouth, "When can we see her?"

"Cody is recovering from a trailer mishap."

The captivated crowd quickly disperse, like rats on a sinking ship. Only our bent ears remain.

"What happened?"

"Cody squeezed her body through the escape door."

Inquisitive expressions of ignorance radiate from Ben's and my faces. Sherrie proceeds to enlighten: "The door in the front of the trailer is meant for people, not horses." Pointing to a nearby trailer, Sherrie shows us the door to which she's referring. It is maybe eighteen inches wide and fifty inches tall. Hardly large enough space for a human to escape, much less a horse. "It must have been a tight squeeze," that's all I can say. What was that mare thinking?

The way we perceive ourselves isn't

necessarily reality.

Thus,

we attempt to do things we really shouldn't.

"Give her a couple more weeks and we'll make it happen. I want to be sure she's all right." Conscientiously, Sherrie delays us. "You may not want her; if not, that's OK." Sherrie knows we're greenhorns, leaving us with one last piece of advice. "If you are serious about purchasing a horse, watch out for horse traders...

"They'll tell you anything to get their horse sold.

You're better off knowing someone

with experience who can help you."

This applies to anything, not just a horse.

(Houses, cars, spouses)

Two weeks pass. "Cody is good to go!"

The three of us meet at the ten acres where Cody resides. What an ideal location to board a horse, adjacent to Van Bibber Park. Cody is fetched from knee-high-grass.

Our eyes cascade over the shimmering, reddish-brown bay sporting about a jet-black mane, tail and legs. Look, white stockings from her hooves to her knees on all fours!

It's love at first sight. Her stunning appearance has me mesmerized. Captured by the poise and presence of this horse, I can't take my eyes off her. My hand slowly gravitates to her delicate face. "She's beautiful," softly stream from my lips. All eyes are fixed on this small-framed horse with a very rotund belly.

Even though we're told she can be feisty, she remains calm. Examination begins of her flawless frame tied to the rail. My hand glides with pleasure over her smooth, supple, reddish-brown hair.

"What a pleasant demeanor. She's very sweet." As if I know these things.

All the horses I've seen have enormous heads and snouts. Cody's features are delicate and refined. Her face is exquisite. A white star rests between her eyes and a snip of white is smudged on her snout. My hand caresses her extraordinary soft nose. It feels luxurious like cashmere. I'm compelled to touch her hairy ears. They flinch with sensitivity, as if I'm annoying her, or she is aware of my touch. I'm not sure which. The muscle mass of this animal is extraordinary. She has a toned rear end, with not an ounce of fat. With great admiration, I comment, "I wish mine was like that!"

I'm not intimidated by her size in the least! This is a first! "Lovely! Just lovely! Do you like her, Sunshine?"

With a sharp smug, Sunshine rolls her eyes and replies,

"Mom, you have to ride a horse to get a feel to see if you like it or not."

"Oh, I was not knowing." Sheepishly I cave to the self-appointed authoritarian. What does Mom know anyway? I'm sure the pre-teen will inform you, "She knows nothing, absolutely nothing! She's from the dark ages you know."

Cody's offspring frolics around in the pasture. It's a mini Cody; a half-pint.

"Cute little thing; is she a year old?" I take a stab at her youth.

Shaking her head with a chuckle, Sherrie responds, "No, she's five. That horse belongs to my friend. She uses her for rodeo."

"Mercy! She is a tiny thing!"

"Don't be deceived by her size,

she's a great little powerhouse!"

"Did I tell you Cody was a broodmare? She and her foal were abandoned by their previous owner. Cody throws extremely small foals, as you can see."

Skills to decode equinese would be handy right about now. What does she mean...throw small foals?

I'm drawn into this incredible abandonment story. Cody must have issues, but who doesn't?

Listen up as Sherrie continues the saga. "One day I received a call from the landlord, asking if I'd take them. He told me the previous owners deserted two horses in the pasture."

Just because one person doesn't want

someone or something

doesn't mean you dispose of it as trash.

Someone else is bound to love

and appreciate what you don't.

Like the credits running after a movie, Sherrie divulges more character, attributes, and dysfunctions. (People aren't the only ones impacted by dysfunction.) "Cody had no prior training. Green broke is all she was until the age of ten."

We listen as curious sponge cakes, sucking up all the gooey caramel Sherrie can drizzle.

"One more thing, Cody doesn't like the whip."

We are all ears.

"In the event you need to use it, you'll have better results using it this way." Sherrie demonstrates how to discreetly shield the three-foot whip from sight.

To duplicate her contortion is a trick in itself! You try it. "Hide the whip behind your back; now make it reappear in front without being visible. Once you've accomplished that exercise, touch the horse with the tip of the whip."

It's complicated, huh? For some reason tying oneself into a knot to hide a rope is bit peculiar and awkward.

"You'll get used to it. It's really not that difficult, Reneé."

"Oh." I find this contortion trick rather confusing.

Sherrie shares Cody's pedigree. "She's a National Show Horse, a mix of Saddlebred and Arabian."

"That explains her delicate face and head. The swan-like arch in her neck is an Arabian characteristic, right?"

"Yes, that's right." Impressed, I'm sure, with my only piece of equine knowledge, Sherrie dollops on the whipped cream. "Cody has points too; she placed 'Best of Show.'" How impressive is that! Whatever that means, I have no idea. It sure sounds impressive, though! Show points, the cherry that sweetens deal!

"I like to think of Cody as being fourteen hands high, but that pushes the envelope a bit." There she goes speaking that equinese again. It all boils down to this -- Cody's a small horse.

A tug on my jacket diverts my attention from horse fixation. Suddenly I hear a young nagging voice, "Mom, I want to ride her!"

"Well, jump on and ride her then."

Sunshine is barely able to wrap her slim legs around the portly belly. Legs stick out as a bow-legged version of the splits!

Is Cody pregnant?

Tickled by Sunshine's awkward riding position and my question, Sherrie chuckles, "No, I haven't ridden or exercised her. She's been lazy, grazing in the pasture. Remember, Cody has been recovering from a trailer incident. A bit stout, huh?"

The anticipated bareback ride begins. The two take off with a waddle, then transition into a slight trot, now a full gallop! The arch in Cody's neck mirrors her high and pretty arched tail. The faster they lope, the more Cody wildly flings her head. Impressively, Sunshine controls this spirited beauty. She rides with authority. This mare is everything we'd hoped for and more. Cody and Sunshine seem well suited for each another.

Cody gallops right to the edge of our feet before an abrupt stop. I jump back to avoid being trampled. After I catch my breath and composure, I ask, "Sunshine, now that you've had a chance to ride, do you like her?"

With a slight up and down motion of her head, bright eyes radiate with an understated sign of approval.

I'm ready to bust a gut with excitement but hold back with a low-key, cool mom, restrained approach, "Sold. Sherrie, will you deliver her?"

Soon after, Cody arrives in a lovely new two-horse slant trailer. It appears to be the Cadillac of trailers. WOW! How impressive! I want one of those.

"It's big and roomy and rides like a dream," Sherrie tells me. "I got a great deal on it too."

I probe, "what does a great deal look like for this beauty of yours?"

"It's a ten-thousand-dollar trailer; I paid three. It's only a year old. A divorce forced the sell."

Envy curls my hair. "That was a great deal you stumbled onto. Tell me more."

"The gentleman turned down my offer at first. I waited and watched. The trailer sat on the corner with a 'for sale' sign for a long time. I waited several more weeks, and then called again. I made the same offer of three-thousand. He took it."

Patience and perseverance have benefits.

Affectionate hugs are exchanged before Sherrie jumps into her truck to leave. Curious eyes follow her down the dirt road. Cody watches her best friend depart. Her reaction to Sherrie's departure is a soulful whinny *"goodbye"*. I find it profoundly moving, as though Cody knows she won't see Sherrie again.

Insight into the tender depths of a horse.

ST

Ride Baby Ride

4

Let me introduce you to Sunshine's Westernaires friend, Savannah. She is a confident little twelve-year-old who boards her horse at the Lazy Heart Ranch. The girls intend to share Savannah's recently acquired four-horse stock trailer to attend events and practices. Like lost puppies, we follow Savannah around the grounds.

Savannah cocks her head, and points downwind with a grin, "There is no indoor plumbing here. We girls have our own one-holer. You know, for your personal business. The riding arena is just beyond the outhouse."

Savannah tosses her long, dark, thick wavy hair about, relishing the position of top dog, wrapping up the tour, "Sunshine, tie Cody up next to my horse. We'll saddle up and ride in the arena."

"Hey, we have a car to unload before the two of you trot off."

Teens are so easily distracted.

They think it's all about them.

My iris-blue compact Corolla was not built to perform as a pickup, but it's amazing the stuff it can hold. Watch as the girls unload the entire collection of brand-new tack from the depths of its trunk. Every Westernaires horse needs a purple and green padded blanket, with coordinating reins and head stall. A charcoal wool blanket follows. We'll use this one under the pretty one. All the pristine grooming supplies trail, which include a couple of brushes, a hoof pick, curry comb, mane detangler, fly spray and a coordinating purple case to help with tool organization. Just when you think this trunk couldn't possibly hold another item, I reach deep to extract a brand spankin' new forty-pound leather saddle wedged in the trunk's rear.

Ah, the sweet smell of rawhide lingers. Can you smell it? It beats any air freshener. "Be careful," as the heavy saddle is handed off to one of the girls. Feet dance to jostle the flailing heavy apparatus over the rail. At this rate, these two will be buff in no time. That is if they don't first knock each other out.

Let's watch the girls show off their grooming skills. Soft bristles flow over horses' backs in the direction the hair grows. Dirt clods fly. Back away from the groomers, or you'll get your eye poked by airborne clods or swinging picks. Look at those girls confidently grab and bend horse legs and dig hooves. The scent of manure fills nasal passages as pedicures advance. Plop, plop, warm steamy horse deposits plummet to our feet. Pretty pungent fragrances when you're not accustomed to it. Nose's curl. At least this one's does.

Savannah warns. "Don't step in it!"

"OOPS! Yuck!" My distorted face reveals disgust as I lift my newly purchased wet boot oozing with freshly deposited dark green moist poop.

"That's what the shovel is for!" Savannah barks, "Don't leave the poop at the rail; clean it up for those who follow behind!"

Yikes, I've been told! I'll not do that again.

Curry combs stumble across tangled dark manes. Blankets fling over horses' backs. Limber girls stretch to retrieve the cinches under bellies as they lace them through the ring on the other side. This tightens up the saddles. In unison, the girls proficiently administer the bit. Metal clashes with teeth. I cringe, although neither the animals nor the girls seem to be bothered. Next in line, the headstall tug-of-war. If it's not held firmly, the bit falls from the horse's mouth. Young fingers gently wrestle to bend furry ears through the holes of the head stalls, and then buckle the bright braided apparatus under the chin. Not too tight, two fingers' width is the rule. It's apparent the girls know what to do.

It's poetic pleasure to witness a couple of twelve-year-olds operate with such efficiency.

Off to the arena. The girls retighten cinches before they mount. How colorful they look, all decked out in their new western wear; the horses, I mean. Two horses, two preteens and a twelve-hundred-acre ranch is a recipe for an exciting adventure.

"Come on, Mom, jump on the back, I'll take you for a ride."

So I do. Safe enough, I figure. My first ride in the arena is doubles with my daughter. I struggle hoisting my big butt over the saddle. What a chore! To use the corral fence in lieu of a stepping stool is next to impossible.

I no more than get on, when Cody abruptly spins around, than jerks and spins the opposite direction. An amusement ride of sorts. where grownups suffer whiplash and kids experience a big thrill. Yes, Cody and Sunshine go one direction and I go the other! Kerplunk!

"O-O-O-O-O-O!" Sucking down sand isn't my idea of fun! Not to mention it's hard on this ole gal's body.

The girls can't help but laugh at me. Not wanting to humiliate me too bad, Sunshine yells, "Come on, Mom! Get back on!"

I pick my bad-self up from the earthen gravel bed, painfully moaning, spitting sand from my teeth and other parts unknown, "You've got to be kidding!"

"Come on, Mom, you have to get back on."

"NO! That hurts!" Disgruntled, I think to myself, these bones are older than you, sweet thing!

My daughter commands me,

"Just get back on the horse

immediately after you take a fall

or you never will!"

Reluctantly, I mount for a second time. Will I survive this learning curve? Mounted for only thirty seconds when Cody violently spins again! As if the first time was for practice. Passionately, I kiss the sand once more.

"O-O-O-O-O-O, my body doesn't like this much," I

mumble. I must be a glutton for punishment. Maybe I've lost all my good sense; that is, if I had any to lose.

"Get back on, Mom!" Sunshine commands.

"I don't want to."

"Come on." With a snappy smile of encouragement from my daughter, I do. Not to be outdone by an adolescent.

She's right.

It would have been a lot easier,

not to have gotten back on.

Less painful, that's for sure.

If I allow a little pain and defeat

Or fear to keep me down,

I won't experience

The life changing adventures

waiting to be found!

Life is like that

when you take a tumble,

leave no room for regret, get back up,

try it again, or you never will.

ST

Pigheaded

5

A horse manual for dummies should be required reading for greenhorns like me. A little knowledge before plunging into the world of equine is a good idea. Horse ownership is not much different than life.

You don't know

what you don't know.

Trial by fire, plunge in and just do it.

What adolescent girl doesn't want a horse? Or a friend to ride with? After school Sunshine and Savannah meet at the ranch decked out in their Westernaires' uniforms. White would not be the color of choice for most parents. Ask the girls, they don't care. They do look sharp in their soon to be soiled pristine pants and shirt. See the crimson "W" monogrammed on the back of their snow-white blouses?

Step back in time, reminiscent of the 1950's. Their hair is pulled back with a red bandana tied behind their heads. The ranch is not the environment for pretty princess attitudes.

Trailering is new for us but old hat for Donald, Savannah's father. Don is easily spotted in a crowd. He's the one with the signature bushy brows, beard and mustache. Twisting his brows, he instructs the eager girls how to load both horses in the trailer. Confident chatter is exchanged between the mini adults. This is Sunshine's first practice since becoming a proud owner. There, they load without a hitch. That was easy. We're off!

The arena is full of parents chatting on the sidelines and kids practicing precision drills. This is such a thrill for us tonight. Cody is easy to spot. Clearly, she is pleased to be with a herd. She's the only bay flinging her head every which way. Look, do you see her? She's the squirrely one. You can spot her easily amongst the fifty or so no-nonsense horses. Cody's white socks help set her apart. Her step appears to be much higher than the others. The rest of the herd is relaxed, you can tell, they have done this routine a thousand times.

It's as if Cody says, *"Look at me. What do you think? Isn't this grand? Am I the prettiest thing out here or what?"*

Horses and riders continuously shift directions. This charging at horses, yet avoiding collision is totally new for Cody. The kids practice complex intertwining wagon wheels and thread-the-needle routines all the time. My Little Bird looks like a pro, so confident and poised, with her eyes on the action-packed, complex maneuvers. Cody's cooperation is imperative. Looking pretty while horsing around just won't fly. Pay attention! That is, if you want to avoid injuries!

Kudos to Sunshine! To control a giddy mare unfamiliar with the intricate routine is a major accomplishment. My daughter shines out there, at least in my eyes.

The clock reads half past eight. Practice is over. Before

heading home, the girls walk their horses to cool them down. Then Savannah loads her horse. Next Cody is given the command to jump into the trailer. Cody has no desire to oblige. This mare wants to remain with her new friends. Who can blame her?

People are the same.

As if who they are

or

what they look like

overrides poor behavior.

Really now?

Cody's obstinate stance speaks volumes.

"*You can go home now; I had a great time. I have new buddies! I'll be fine. Don't worry about me. I'll stay with the herd!*"

The girls try to coax Cody into the trailer, receiving absolutely no cooperation. The light of day is gone. Headlights diminish as the last car drives off the lot. All the other kids have loaded their horses and are long gone. The parking lot is deserted and dark, except for the soft moonlight, two horses, two dads, two girls and me.

Reluctant to enter the trailer, Cody just stands there looking at us. Is she afraid of the dark; does she have night blindness?

Don and Ben attempt to pull the temperamental mare into the trailer with a rope tied around her neck. This measure seems extreme and cruel to me. Cody doesn't like it much either. Her bright eyes bulge in the moonlight; mine join in, as I'm introduced to the body language of a flamin' furious mare. Cody displays defiance from her core, as if to say, *"Go ahead, push me, pull me, make me, you can try all you want. I'll outlast every one of you!"*

Our effort is fruitless.

It's nearly ten o'clock. We're exasperated. "Cody, we don't have all night! The girls have school tomorrow, and we have work!"

What do you do in a case like this? Somebody needs to do something, anything. I'm too green to say anything. For Pete's sake, don't just stand there looking bewildered -- do something!

Out of desperation, the dreaded whip is brought out. All hell breaks loose. Into the darkness Cody belts out a distressful whinny for help. The whites of her eyes shine like spotlights. Hooves dance back and forth in anxiety. Options are limited for a horse tied to the rear of the trailer. The rope is anchored to a hook. The night is now a blur of raw emotions. Out of mounting frustration someone thinks whipping her into submission will cause compliance. Instead, Cody becomes enraged! **She is mad!** The rope breaks loose as front legs spring straight up in the air, ready for a fight! God spare the one below!

Does a good beating

encourage you to do what you've been told?

I suppose some have been trained

to only respond at the threat of a beating.

Do you see something wrong with this picture?

"BRING IT ON, ALL OF YOU!" Cody protects her stance.

BANG! Hooves crash down on the trailer's rooftop. The abrupt collision echoes throughout the fairgrounds. Cody is so high in the air she loses balance, flips over and lands hard on her back!

This is horrifying to watch! I'm so upset. Tears stream down my cheeks, sobbing in pain. In disbelief I helplessly look on. I have no experience to assist either Cody or the handlers.

What a disturbing predicament!

I'm visibly shaken. I cry out, "Is she all right!?" Sunshine walks over to comfort me in the dark.

"Mom, she has to learn who's boss.

Cody must get in the trailer.

She can't get away with this!"

I find little comfort in her words, but...

Tremendous insight into the adult

arising within my child.

Here we are, scratching our heads, hands on hips, as eyes exchange distressed glances. Tension and disbelief fill the night air. Eleven o'clock silently creeps up. No one knows what to do.

"Help, God. We need help." I softly weep.

An idea about the caretaker living on the fairgrounds comes to someone. "Maybe Jim can help," a tired voice is heard in the dark. "Savannah, run and get Mr. Sullivan, please."

Off she bolts. Hopefully Mr. Sullivan is home. Several minutes later, pulled from bed, disheveled Jim comes to our rescue. He senses our level of frustration is off the charts.

Calmly, Jim questions, "What have you done so far?" He

never spanks us for our poor handling of the situation. The night has been traumatic enough. We are grateful to be spared additional pain.

A man with some real horse sense comes not only to deliver us, but Cody as well. The serenity Jim brings is a breath of fresh air to our calamity. He is really good with Cody. A godsend. A fresh face not associated with the horrifying event doesn't hurt either.

"Sunshine, this is what I want you to do," Jim calmly instructs. "Walk into the trailer with a little grain, a little hay, a little coaxing and a gentle voice."

Without hesitation, Cody follows Sunshine right into the trailer. I burst into tears. Each of us expels a huge sigh of relief!

Jim obviously knows what he's doing. He's the deliverer of peace to our storm.

SUCCESS! MISSION ACCOMPLISHED!

We have been struggling to load a pigheaded horse for over two hours.

What she needs is a trainer, but who can afford that? Besides, she knows how to load. A trainer is not contacted. We never look into one. After all, a trainer is bound to be expensive. Funds are limited, I justify in my mind.

Revenge for use of the whip runs rampant. Every trick in Cody's playbook is implemented to create grief. No longer is ownership a pleasure, rather, a chore and drudgery. Cody remains eager to attend class, but never cooperates for the return trip. The weekly trek to Westernaires becomes an exasperating ordeal. Although not verbalized, I'm certain Savannah's dad wishes he never offered to trailer this temperamental mare.

The battle of wills converges every week. Does she not like where she lives? Does she enjoy tormenting us? Anxiety disorder? Hormonal? Questions flood my mind to determine and justify irrational behavior. Why does Cody create such a production every trip home?

Is this what a drama queen looks like?

Who knows what goes on in the mind of a horse? One can only speculate. Like people, their attitude, behavior and body language speaks volumes.

Sunshine is frustrated with the whole thing. "I don't want to do this anymore. Mom, I quit!"

"Quit? You can't just quit!"

"I quit!"

Oh, my heart sinks. I'm sickened. Yet I understand her frustration. Cody is relentless! Sunshine's life is made miserable by a horse. It's all over. If this was what Cody wanted, she won.

Sunshine has no interest in returning to the ranch. The emotional disconnect becomes apparent. It kills me to leave Cody in a stall the size of a phone booth without exercise or human contact. Sunshine's apathy profoundly saddens me. She would never abandon her dog.

Horses and teenagers,

can both be pigheaded.

Not always willing to embrace

the training process to improve skills.

Why is this?

Sunshine won't budge. For two weeks Cody wastes away, not even a visit. I just can't stand it any longer.

"SUNSHINE, CODY IS TOO GOOD OF AN ANIMAL TO ALLOW HER TO ROT IN A STALL! IF YOU WON'T RIDE HER, THEN I WILL!"

On that note, I storm off to the ranch. I did not raise my daughter to be a quitter! This angry mom is not the least bit pleased.

You don't quit just because

things don't go your way or smoothly.

That's life!

Put on your big girl panties and get over it!

Pigheaded Friend

Do you hate them?

Kick and abuse?

Or

Accept them for who they are,

As we hope they do for us in return

Warts, farts and all

We all have it within

It emerges differently in each of us

Do you recognize it in yourself?

It's easy to see it in others

But rarely does the looking glass reveal

it to ourselves

Oh, that deceptive mirror--

We adore and embrace

TV

In The Saddle

6

Following my explosion over my daughter's sorrowful decision to quit, I reach out to my single girlfriend from church who possesses tremendous confidence; it's the way we roll. Both of us are in our late thirties. Neither Deb nor I have any riding experience, or if she does, it's a big secret. Still, we are both very capable women who are up to the task of figuring out this equine stuff.

In my recently acquired equine wisdom, I believe it necessary to build connection between horse and rider. So, Deb and I bury apple treats in our pockets. We walk around the arena just to see if Cody will follow. Without further effort on our part, a discerning nose closely follows alongside. Dummies we are not; we know she's nibbling through our clothes at the hidden treats. Bribery is a wonderful form of manipulation. Cookies are a brilliant way to create a bond! Go figure. Horses have a sweet tooth. But don't give a horse chocolate. I'm warning you, just don't do it!

Deb's long black hair waves in the breeze as she extends the invitation, "Reneé, I'll watch if you want to go first."

With a hearty "Okay," I oblige.

Deb holds the reins as I prepare to mount on the left side of Cody using the slick technique I learned in Westernaires. Stand in the opposite direction of the horse and twist the stirrup around. Hold onto the horn; insert left foot into the stirrup. This procedure enables more options for survival in the event your horse flinches, does a hip-hop dance and bolts around the arena, like right now! Before I can get my right leg swung over the saddle, we fly! FAST! Call it a death-defying trick ride! You've seen the circus act. The crowd gasps and springs to their feet in the grandstands! Spectators roar at the outlandish trick on steroids. The brave trick rider takes a lap around the arena with one foot caught in the stirrup, while her body flaps against the side of the horse like a rag doll. That kind of exciting trick ride! Everything happens at such an alarming rate.

Oddly, when in danger,

our minds are capable of processing

at an accelerated rate,

faster than the speed of real time.

This gives opportunity

to make appropriate decisions.

Strange how it works,

these are my logical thoughts

as Cody pursues her sweet victory lap.

If I choose to let go,

my foot could remain caught in the stirrup

and I will dangle off the side of the horse

or be dragged underfoot.

Possibly trampled on!

Talk about a scared horse!

This could get ugly.

Or

I can hang on and pray for the best!

Under distress, options are quickly assessed as my heart races, scared out of its wits! I don't have the strength or wherewithal to pull myself up over the saddle as the center of gravity is much too low. A highly-trained professional trick-rider holds onto a very special saddle horn built for outrageous stunts like this. This saddle is not equipped with that trick horn, nor is a professional trick rider in the saddle. I think I'll take my chances. Reneé, hold on for all you're worth! Don't let go!

Adrenaline rushes while auburn hair lightly brushes the dusty billowed ground. Terrified eyes watch a leg and arm flail as the highly incompetent rider dangerously bounces off the side of a spirited runaway.

Cody impresses the imaginary cheering masses on their feet with a blistering fast victory lap!

I wonder if this horrifying ride qualifies for the "cowgirl up badge?" Although the crowd is merely a figment of my vivid imagination, the rest is dead on accurate. Scary, huh?

The celebration finale is over. Cody relaxes and comes to

an abrupt stop, as if nothing ever happened. Not for fame or fortune, do I ever care for a repeat performance, NOT EVER!

Deb frantically rushes toward us, "Are you all right?"

Weak at the knees I struggle to untangle myself from the convoluted web of legs and tack before I'm able to dismount. "Yeah, I'm fine; how did I look?" I break out into nervous laughter mingled with an occasional snort!

"You are good! At least you held on! I'll say you look like a real cowgirl out there. It was queasy to watch." Uncertain about my true welfare, Deb repeats several times, "Are you sure you're OK?"

Slightly amused by the unsettling event, this bobble-head doll acknowledges the question, "I believe an instructor is in order!"

Deb fails to see the humor. "Do ya think?" as she swishes her small frame. I, on the other hand, find humor in the most unusual places. Call me strange if you like. It isn't the first time I've heard it.

Over the next several days, options for a trainer come to mind. My savvy twelve-year-old could be a possibility, but role reversal may not be such a great idea. Hmm, I need someone with a bit more experience, and maybe some age under their belt would be beneficial.

Over the years, I've seen a lot of riders to admire. After all, Kevin Costner rides, so did John Wayne. It can't be all that hard. These guys are just actors, right? If they can do it, then so can I!

My mission: Seek out someone to teach me how to really ride.

~~~~

Shirley boards her old flea-bitten mare here at the ranch. I've noticed her on occasion, as not many riders are here on Mondays and Tuesdays. An accomplished rider in her fifties, she is a wee little gal. Her tousled long gray hair protrudes from her rugged well-worn cowgirl hat.

Destiny awaits... Monday and Tuesday are my days off. Shirley and I have become somewhat friendly. I think maybe, just maybe, she's the one who could show me the ropes! All I have to do is ask. The worst that can happen is she says "no."

"Shirley, will you help? Can you teach me to ride?"

She agrees, and we begin the process of grooming and learn the names of saddle parts. What do I care about parts? How to mount safely; it isn't the mount I struggle with. Well... OK, maybe I could use some help with mounting. Shirley lays the foundation for all the necessary things that don't interest me in the least.

"Aren't we ever going to ride?" I mutter under my breath.

"Never hold onto the horn," Shirley passionately instructs, "It will throw you off balance."

"Never? Yikes!" The horn's my source of security. Without it, I could fall off!

"OK, let's saddle up and take Cody into the arena," Shirley directs. "Let's see what she's made of!"

"Oh, I'm fully aware of Cody's antics. That's why I need help, Shirley."

We make our way to the corral. Like a schoolgirl on her first date, sweaty palms and cuticles gnawed down to the knuckles tell all. I have already spent ample time tossed from the back of this spirited mare. I'm not really a glutton for punishment, rather, I'm tenacious. I refuse to allow Cody to get the best of me. She has met her match.

"Don't be scared; Cody can sense fear." I never told Shirley I was afraid. Either she is intuitive, or my face is a dead giveaway. Or maybe it's my gnawed off fingernails.

Does fear produce a scent?

How does it smell?

Maybe it has a body language all its own.

Whatever it is,

Humans and animals both recognize it.

Cynically, I think out loud, "Yeah, let me flip off the switch. Do I have control over fear?"

Weeks of training transpire. The drama queen unleashes her bad-self to demonstrate her favorite stunt. No doubt, her antics are meant to impress. Cody is one great entertainer. Unfortunately for me, I'm the greenhorn left sucking up sand.

"Let's try it again." It's my privilege to stretch Shirley's ability to problem solve. I have no doubt we are a challenge. If she had to do it all over, she might have turned down my request for instruction. Shirley digs deep to equip me with skills to overcome goofy behaviors.

"*Touchdown!*" The sassy bay runs a celebratory victory lap, kicking up her heels in pride over her rider's elimination! Joy to her world! This mare obviously finds gratification from her newly established routine. I've become Cody's sick pleasure. And to think, I'm a willing participant! Once again, I pick my bad-self from the ground and shake sand from parts unknown. I need therapy, that's all there is to it.

Generally, the ranch owner is doing business at his kitchen table, keeping a watchful eye on the screen monitor for suspicious activity. Today, however, Marvin, a well-seasoned gentleman whose belly over-hangs his britches, happens to be standing at the corral rail observing us. As I reflect, I wonder if it was a conspiracy on Shirley's behalf to acquire Marvin's insight to keep this gal upright. There is no doubt; I need all the help I can get! Shirley must be frustrated too.

Marvin watches as once again, Cody successfully plants my already pitted face into the sand. How humiliating. Graciously, Marvin shares his lifesaving advice.

"Reneé, plant half your weight in the saddle,

the other half in the stirrups.

Keep your heels down."

(Life is all about balance, isn't it?)

WOW! Does that ever make a difference! With hands raised I shout out, "Praise God, intervention has come!"

Learning to master balance

enables us to ride those unforeseen

"Dances of life".

Dancing with a fickle horse is a little awkward at first. It takes a while to find rhythm with your partner. Perseverance pays off. The dance becomes a delightful experience when partners are synchronized. Rest your derriere in the saddle instead of slapping against it. In case you missed the key, put half your weight in the stirrups with heels down. Begin to feel the gait of your partner. When your rise and fall movement syncs with the horse, you become a single unit working together. It's the same with ballroom dancing. Let that man lead you on the dance floor, girlfriend! Gentlemen, she needs a strong lead. Step up to the plate.

Only one can lead the dance,

or

it's not a pretty sight!

Later the lead will be mine, but for today, it's Cody's. At least now I'm more equipped to keep from flying off. Pranks that intentionally throw me off are no longer successful! Not regularly, anyway.

When I purchased this feisty mare, there was no indication of our similarities. Strong-willed, spirited, determined and some might add strange. (I'll leave that conclusion up to you). Our resemblances make the challenge more compelling.

Horses and people are a lot alike!

It's a competitive battle of wills at this point, purely a game of skill, wits, tenacity and determination.

Who will be the victor?

Cody's behavioral patterns are out of the ordinary for a horse. Mine are outside the box as well. One thing I know for sure, expect the unexpected!

We're a great match!

"Bring it on, Cody. Bring it on!

Cody Takes Flight

7

Have you ever argued with yourself? How is the winner determined? I embrace a good scuffle on occasion. If we are honest, most prefer the top dog position. Lately, my battle stretches me. Should I ride beyond the corral boundary? A thousand acres stare back, calling my name, yet I stay within the comfort of the arena. It's familiar, you know, comfortable.

Staring past the fence line, I try to convince myself, "You'll like it."

"I don't wanna go," bellows the snipped retort.

I try a different approach, appealing to my fun side, "Self, it'll be adventurous!"

"But it's not safe; there are no railings to hold this crazy horse back. You know how she is!"

"But there is a whole new world to explore. It knows your name. It calls you."

Relentless goes the argument.

Consoling myself, "Self, when it's time to venture out, you'll do so. Don't let a little apprehension stop you."

"Give it a try!"

"Thanks, but not today."

"Ooooo..." Well, I guess that settled that! I lost!

Horses, kids, old people

and everyone in between

don't like being pushed into things

or

for that matter, told what to do.

Most of the time, I accept a new challenge. I'm not one to shy away, but I don't like being forced. This is scary stuff for this greenhorn.

"Stop nagging me!"

Funny, nagging thoughts arise to challenge a decision already made.

There is no sense in fighting or

becoming hardened to the process.

Embrace the things you cannot change.

God puts within us a GPS
to equip us for the journey we are to blaze.

The voice within finally persuades me to explore the ranch. Apprehension creates delay. "What's the sense of stashing toys? Or hiding a sports car in the garage for a rainy day? Just to have it and not use it? Really? How much fun is derived from that?" For me to ride Cody beyond the comfort of the corral is the same principle.

"Self! You should know by now...."

Our conscience is our guide.

Don't be scared!

Pay attention.

Don't procrastinate,

or opportunities will pass you by.

Empowered with courage, sort of, today is the day to ride beyond comfort. Yes! I choose to do this. Yes, today I will stretch myself. Yes, I am prepared. I have purchased all the right gear for the inaugural ride. Flashy as a magazine cover - being the colorful city gal that I am, fashion reigns supreme. After all, it's all about the coordinated look, right? I'm decked out in my new full-length, oiled Australian outback duster. My auburn curls, naturally kissed by the sun and painted by the tint brush, emerge from beneath the newly purchased Aussie hat. I'm struttin' brand new two-toned, Ariat lace-up cowgirl boots, built to kick some bootie. "Dress for success," "they" always say. Whoever "they" are. Will this new air of confidence glue me to the saddle? I can only hope.

Cody looks sharp too, freshly brushed coat glistens beneath the saddle, adorned with recently acquired genuine leather reins and gentle bit.

Persistence is standard equipment for both of us. Sometimes wills collide, for a pleasing mix of adventure, exploration and competition.

Cody is not a motorcycle, although as dangerous. She's unpredictable. I can't turn her off with a switch or shut her down in the event I lose control.

Shirley's voice plays in the back of my head, "If she won't listen or is too quick for you, bend her neck around in a circle. She'll slow down."

Lookin' great! Intimidation meets us at the gate, will the fashionista overcome what lurks on the other side? I gaze between the rusty rails of the closed cattle gate. Palms wet with perspiration, legs tremble.

Never have cattle hung out at the gate. They are always elsewhere. But not today! It's the day we choose to venture out and would ya look! Threatening creatures clothed in fur, guard the gate. That's right! The only entry. Great, just great!

Don't let that stop you, girl. Suck it up! Don't be a chicken. It's time...

Take a deep breath ~

Gingerly I press open the daunting pasture gate ~

Jostling a thousand-pound animal for position through a two-foot opening is a tight squeeze! Anything to prevent being the center of a stampede suits me well. Whew! Is it gutsy to mount goofy surrounded by her despised enemy? My heart flutters. Take a pause ... breathe... mount... squeeze those thighs. It's exciting and daunting, all at the same time. Ebony cow eyes stare us down as we stealthily tap dance through the herd as one might tread on a bed of cobras. Hopefully, we will survive with bragging rights!

"Don't look them in the eye," I warn Cody.

If cows could be annoyed, this is it. Not willing to yield an inch. Cody's head and tail are upright and rigid. Her ears perk up, her nostrils flare, and intimidating snorts begin.

"OOOOO, Cody, just ignore those old cows. They won't hurt you. Cattle don't eat horses. Relax girl, relax." I should take my own advice. This is my first episode with a herd of fuzzy fur balls. I have no idea what to anticipate or do in a pinch. In the movies, livestock automatically part at the presence of horses like the Red Sea did for Moses. Obviously, these cows didn't read the script, or they'd move over as we pass by.

"They're gonna eat me!" Cody snorts her way through the herd.

Nervously, I chuckle, "Act goofy if you want. You don't fool me!" Admittedly, I too wonder what the fur balls will do. Will I get bumped off by a ballistic mare or trampled by a herd of fur?

Jitters emerge from down under. Perspiration froths Cody's saturated chest. I pull heavy on the reins, fearful she'll explode. Cody twists and distorts the beautiful dressage sidestep. It's hysterical; that is, if I'm not the one braced in the saddle.

Painfully, we dance through the herd without mishap. Tense muscles relax. No furry creatures follow. Together we exhale a huge sigh of relief.

I think she covers her fears,

acting dominant.

You know,

like people do when they feel threatened.

Seemingly tough on the surface,

masking fear hidden within.

Phew, that was an ordeal! We barely survived the cow induction. In a short distance, lies the intimidating ditch. It measures approximately twenty-five to thirty inches wide and maybe, just maybe, nine inches deep. It's nothing.

Cody abruptly stops!

"It's the scariest trickle of water I've ever seen!" Rolling my eyes, I scorn, "Really, Cody? You act as though we stumbled upon the Grand Canyon's rim."

Rocking set in motion. Several minutes pass. We rock back and forth, building up steam, I can feel it. Swift as a deer, we take flight and plunge over the little ditch!

OH, MY WORD! SHE'S AFRAID OF WATER!

Finesse and containment are not my finer attributes. Belly laughter spews forth with a hilarious snort! I tell you; this snorting thing is contagious. Beware! It could happen to you!

"Cody, you are too funny!"

Two fears confronted and overcome in a single day! How strenuous is that? Intense, I tell you, intense! This horse is a hoot!

Fear can be dealt with head-on;

You will survive!

Usually, the circumstances are not

nearly as big as they appear in one's mind.

We rocked it! Conquerors of treacherous ditches and scarry fur balls we are. With a newly found air of confidence, we settle into a casual groove.

~~~~

A week passes before Shirley and I join up. "Reneé, are you up for the challenge of a real ride?"

"OH, YES!" Eager at the notion of a real ride! "Let's go!" Enthusiastic words slip right pass these thick lips of mine before I can wrap my head around what I just agreed to.

You know,

this speaking before thinking,

can really get you into a lot of trouble.

I should know!

We are in motion when blind excitement turns to trepidation. We tried this last week. Fur balls could be present. A horse can run forever in an endless pasture. How intimidating, yet exciting!

"Yeah, let's go!" Without reservations, I climb on board Shirley's harebrained idea.

Confidently, we travel at a brisk trot. I can tell you, Cody is delighted to be released from arena restraints, and with a riding partner too! Her gait has a pleasant bounce, smooth and rhythmic. Hooves lift high in a prance. We are transitioning into a real team. I'm moving with her body, connecting to her gait. It's a proud moment in a cowgirl wannabe's life. Following Cody's lead, I keep my hiney planted in the saddle to prevent a faceplant repeat. No longer do we work as separate units, but as one.

Shirley leads us to a dirt road peppered with stones the size of softballs. "I love to run here. There's a lot less rocks than the rest of the pasture. Reneé, we're going to haul butt through this section. Are you ready?"

I stammer with uncertainty, "O-O-O-O-OK," my eyes twice their natural size. What have I gotten myself into?

The leather reins are now supple from the moisture in my palms. The chicken challenge, ready or not, is here! Do you recall your first roller coaster ride? The queasy tummy, shut your eyes and scream moment? That's how I feel right now! At the same time, I don't want to miss a thing.

Obstacles can distract

and sabotage the journey.

The imaginary green flag is dropped! With a swift kick to the ribs, we open up the horses. It's a full-blown race! With incredible speed we trample whatever's beneath! Hooves clamor against stones. All our manes resemble to a billowing cloud of dirt. Nervous perspiration gives way to pearly white teeth.

What a thrill!

YES! Triumph wrapped in overwhelming satisfaction is **unbelievable!** And to think the saddle and I did not part company! Laughter explodes!

"YEE-HAW! Is this fun or what?"

Quietly, Shirley acknowledges with a twinkle in her eye and a big grin on her dusty face. My instructor now has a **bona fide** riding partner. Euphoria invades my space. I think... I'm a real cowgirl now!

Shirley familiarizes me with the open range. "There are a

lot of rocks out there. Be careful. The horses might stumble." She introduces me to the roaming herd. These horses belong to fellow boarders. They must catch them in order to ride.

"Twelve hundred acres is a whole lot of land to look for a horse. How do they do it?" I probe.

Shirley's speculates. "I don't know. Not very often is my guess." The guided tour continues. "This beautiful gelding is Skip. He belongs to Boots."

"Skip is gorgeous," I admire. "You can't help but admire the buff-and-oyster paint job he struts."

"He's independent, too. You'll never see him with the others. He's used solely for hunting; that's it. Boots never rides him. He has another horse, a red Quarter Horse, thus his name, 'Red.' Red wanders with the herd. You'll rarely see the two together."

Spellbound, I savor to every expedition detail, as a cool drink on a steamy hot afternoon.

"The ranchers don't like you messin' with the cattle. Don't ever chase them." Shirley resumes familiarizing me with the rules and lay of the land. "This is a great waterin' hole. That is, when there's water in it." There is, so we stop to give the horses an opportunity to drink. They share no interest in the idea. So... this is what is meant by the old saying, "You can lead a horse to water, but you can't make him drink." It's true. You can't make a horse drink. No matter how desperately you think they need one. It's a funny thing...

People are similar.

You can direct them,

but you can't make them

do anything they don't want to do.

No matter how badly you want it for them.

The ranch is a fascinating place to explore--rolling hills, rocks, sagebrush and dried cow patties are telling signs of cattle whereabouts. Land, lots of land with horses. Only one other house is nestled in the trees over the ridge. The majestic Rockies as the scenic gateway to the west adds flavor to our experience. This incredibly rich sight is appreciated but often taken for granted by the local natives, of which I am one; almost, anyway.

Embrace the sense of peace as it brushes your cheek. There is no lack of quiet. Leave city noise and toxic fumes behind. This urbanite could learn to love this lifestyle. What a great form of mental therapy. I can use some peace in my life right now, as my household displays a bit of drama.

The informative and tranquil tour is concluded. We return to the same path we trampled earlier.

With a twinkle in her eye and a grin of anticipation on her face, Shirley asks in high expectation, "Do you want to race?"

"Race? Wow! Sure!" Feeling frisky, I guess.

Once a routine is established with a horse, they remember it. The memory of a horse is amazing. They've got the routine down. Horses intuitively know what's expected. They do what they're trained to do. You know, like children and pets.

Here we are. This is the place. Open up and run like you stole something is the routine. So, we do! This time is different. We must've stolen somethin' really expensive! We are haulin'! Faster than fast! To control Cody is useless, partially due to my lack of experience, partly due to the thrill of it all!

"O-O-O-O-O-O...EEEEEEEK!"

With reckless abandonment, we gallop across the rocks blistering fast! My eyes swell to the size of softballs, ready to pop out of their sockets! Exhilaration and fear overtake common sense. I feel a lot less frisky right about now!

Self-preservation at its finest; my fingers grip the saddle horn, embedding permanent sweaty prints into the leather. Now, I know I've been told not to grab the horn. Don't think I forgot. I've got to hold on to something! I'm scared spitless! The saddle horn is a life saving device! I will not be denied!

Feel the thrust of a plane accelerate? That's us, we are airborne. Houston, we have liftoff! Cody's wings come from nowhere. I didn't know horses had wings! But they do. Her legs tuck under her belly like the wheels of a plane.

I never felt the ground beneath.

No bouncing... smooth as glass... inconceivable...

EXHILARATING! INCREDIBLE!

A retreat from crisis mode, I indulge in this perpetual surreal utopia. Time stands still, while these few seconds are forever sweetly etched in my soul.

That beautiful moment, that surreal experience... well, straightaway is shattered. Flashes of reality jolt me back in the saddle! Reneé, this is dangerous! I mean really dangerous. **Danger! Warning! Don't panic!** Hold on for the ride! Balance yourself! Stay in the saddle. Don't scream!

"O-O-O-O-O-O-O-O-O!"

This is one of those slow-motion moments. I'm thinking every move through, as if in no hurry. Rationalization finds a new pinnacle. Remain calm, don't panic. Use your head, I reason. Focus, Reneé, keep those heels down. Keep your weight in your stirrups, fear not! Balance, Reneé, stay balanced. Hold on for all you're worth! My mind kicks into sheer survival mode, slow motion style.

Our flight soars off the path at record speed, maybe forty miles an hour. You may not think forty sounds fast, but trust me, when hooves don't touch the ground and you have no control nor protection of any sort, forty is blazin'! Out of control we race. Adrenaline flows. My chest pounds. Will I live to tell the outcome? Out of desperation, words escape these lips of mine. Muted or screaming, I don't recall, "GOD HELP ME!" My skills to maneuver a runaway horse headed straight toward that rock-infested hillside are slightly deficient!

Remain calm.

Think.

It is imperative for survival.

"Yikes!" I snap tight on the reins. "**CODY, listen to me! Get a grip!**"

We could stumble, fall, and both be injured. I could hit my head, or even worse, experience sudden death. This might end my illustrious riding career before it barely begins.

"**Slow down, Cody, slow down!**" The harder I tug on the reins, the less she gives heed. This moment of insubordination is alarming at best. Cody's hydraulic system seems to be jammed! Finally, her wings of flight slow down just enough to cause hooves to stumble, spilling over rocks.

And I thought high speed was scary!

We leave Shirley in the dust. Scared out of my wits, we proceed straight down the hill! Normally, I traverse like a skier snowplowing downhill, at an angle, to slow down the pace.

BUT there is nothing normal about this adventure!

In a blink of an eye, we stop at the corral gate.

Not sure how one cuts through air faster than sound, but what an exhilarating experience! I roll off the horse, barely able to stand, expecting the collapse that never comes. Quivering legs resemble limp noodles. The pounding in my chest is deafening. I'm thinkin' I'll blow up. It's a good day to be alive and unscathed! Uncontrollable laughter mingles with an infectious snort!

"WOW! CODY! Was that ever a blast!"

A ride to remember! The chicken buried within will never consider such a ride again. Truth be told, deep in my subconscious, the thrill calls for a repeat performance!

Fifteen minutes later, Shirley and her old gray mare saunter to the stalls. We never speak of the race. She might have been mad about her mare's inability to keep up. I sure didn't want to flaunt the petrifying victory.

Mercy! My body has found new muscles. You would think my calves would hurt, but no, it's my shins! OH, are they ever screaming!

I find this experience to be quite profound and highly connected to the capers of my teenage daughter.

While Cody is having the time of her life,

doing her own thing,

she is dangerously out of control,

putting not just herself in danger,

but others as well.

Hmm,

like people of the teenage type.

Cody

My beautiful spirited mare

What a teacher you are

Out of control

Dangerous at times

Delight to my soul

Therapy to my heart

A tool of reflection

A lifetime of pleasure

May your lessons

Never stop teaching

My beautiful spirited mare

RB

Grooming

8

Tied up at the OK Corral, Cody patiently waits to be groomed. I brush and bathe her mane and tail with sweet smelling spray. She swishes her glamorous knot-free tail with pride. Her ebony mane glistens, the envy of any female. Next, brush the chunks of dirt clods from underneath. Cody vents frustration as she administers a sporadic shoulder nip. When it comes to the hooves, she willingly lifts each leg automatically, handing each hoof over on request. *"Here, let me help you."* She's certainly well-trained. I rest her lower leg on my thigh, which works well for balance.

Rarely does Cody freak out at sudden noises or moving objects. What an agreeable, calm little horse. A model of good manners, most generally, anyway. I experience cooing moments on occasion, this being one of them. While my back faces Cody, she presses her delicate head between my shoulder blades, rubbing her face hard against me. It could be her sassy way of letting me know I'm annoying her, but I choose to believe it's her way of expressing deep affection. Call me delirious if you want, living in a fantasy world; so be it. I happen to like my world.

Savannah, my newly appointed sassy teenage instructor, purchased a pair of clippers at a yard sale. "Try using these; they should be good for trimming chin whiskers as well as the fetlock hair (the hair above her hooves). No sense in ruining a new pair of clippers for this dirty old job."

Savannah demonstrates clipper how-to's. So as not to startle her, turn the clippers on in the horse's line of vision. Curiously, Cody listens and observes the clatter of blades. Savannah warns, "Don't be scared, Cody," as she gently caresses the backside of the blades over the bay's neck. The motor purrs as blades travel down her legs. "Cody needs to know the clippers won't harm her." Savannah hands over the blades, "OK, you're on your own, have fun." Sassy locks whirl as Savannah returns to horse business of her own.

My first target is the soft mink area under her chin. I babble away, "Cody, you will look lovely after I shave off this goatee!" Four inches of coarse black hair floats like a feather. That was easy and uneventful. No cuts, no bites or attitude, a sure sign of team building. I am so pleased with our progress.

"My, Cody, you sure look better!" I exclaim, as I step back to admire the completed task. I had no idea what a little trim would do for a horse's appearance or I would have done it sooner.

"Next! Let's tackle that fine, furry, feather-lookin' hair at the back side of your hooves. Savannah graciously pointed out; those fetters need attention."

I stand directly behind Cody, face her hind end, elevate

her left leg and hold it between my legs for stability. "Let's get this fluffy hair off you. You'll will be the envy of all the temperamental mares."

The first stroke is smooth as silk. I stand back to observe my handiwork. "Looks pretty good but needs more." I resume the same position for a second pass with the clippers.

No sooner than the blades crossover, this body catapults through the air like a rocket shot from a cannon! That's right, airborne!! Twenty feet away, dazed and stunned, I find myself flat on my back! Excruciating pain rushes to my left shin. Peg-legged I stand up without putting any weight on the injury.

"O-O-O-O-O, man that hurts!"

That's not how you treat

someone you love.

Maybe I need to reevaluate

our love relationship, girlfriend!

I gimp up the stairs into the dusty tack room. It's the trailer where everyone stores their saddles and supplies. I pull down unscathed britches to assess the severity of the injury. I know it's serious. My shin swells like a balloon. How many shades of purple can span over nine inches? It isn't a pretty sight and the pain is horrendous! It'll make a real cowgirl out of ya, that's for darn sure!

By myself in the dimly lit trailer, with no one to help, I question what to do? I process my options.

Option one: seek medical attention immediately.

Option two: pray.

God has been teaching me about praying over my

injuries. By now I've experienced a couple of them. OK, more than a couple, really, quite a few, this being the worst.

Several scriptures flood my heart, riveting my soul with a call to action. Reneé, speak to your mountain.[1] The Word says to "Lay hands on the sick and they will recover."[2]

"If two agree touching anything you ask, it shall be done."[3] Agree with the Word, for there is no one else here to agree with. Don't pay any attention to what it looks like. The Word says, "The just shall walk by faith not by sight,"[4] and besides, "nothing is impossible to those who believe."[5] **Get busy believing!** Lay hands on your leg and pray. Your very livelihood depends on it!

One might ask, how does all this come to mind in the middle of a crisis? Didn't you panic? Amazing how you're able to tap into knowledge on demand. In a split second the brain sorts through stored information to make a flash decision. At least that's my take on the matter.

Panic comes when there

is no knowledge to pull from.

You cannot act upon what you do not know.

What an opportunity to make the instructions of the ancient book my reality, not just words on a page. To put the wisdom to use, I ask myself, "Do you believe it, or don't you?" This is not the time to doubt if it's true or not. Don't just stand there looking at your stiff swollen leg, girl! "It's time to put what you believe into action!" With conviction I announce, **"Do what you know to do!** Take authority as Jesus taught you! Command the mountain of pain to align with healing."

---

[1] Mark 11:24; [2] Mark 16:18; [3] Matthew 18:19; [4] 2 Corinthians 5:7; [5] Matthew 17:20

Get to praying.

You know God heals.

Practice

what you know and believe!

It's easy to believe in something

when you're not in crisis.

The question everyone is confronted with

at some time in their life is,

do you practice what you believe?

Or do you just have knowledge?

Think about it.

I grab my throbbing shin and with authority speak to it, **"I command bruising, pain, swelling and any repercussions, in the name of Jesus, be gone!"**

"There!" With resolve, I hoist up my pants and hobble back to the hitching post, where Cody remains unruffled and relaxed, anticipating my return.

This concludes clipper class #101. I refuse to allow a little pain to stop me from enjoying what I came to do.

"Cody, let's saddle up and ride!"

My shin continues to throb as we ride. I refuse to come into agreement with the pain, only the healing. I praise and thank God for the healing. I'm stubborn that way. I knew this characteristic was good for something!

Well, here it is,

staring me in the face,

the goodness of stubbornness revealed.

Within an hour, Cody and I return to the corral; the pain has subsided. I gimp up the stairs. Return to the tack room; pull down my britches to check the status of my shin bone. The bruising has all disappeared and the swelling is almost gone.

Cody kicked dead center of my shin bone. The bone doesn't feel broken. How can this be? It appears to be only a slight scrape to the skin. Wow! These eyes just witnessed a miracle!

Exercise your believer;

God is awesome!

Far too often we allow our eyes

to dictate what is possible.

It took a year for the tenderness to totally leave, a subtle reminder of the miracle I received. Miraculously, I never walked with a limp or missed work. I didn't share my story but with a few. I figure most would think I'm crazy or not believe it, but trust me, it happened!

In hindsight, those clippers were probably dull and pulled her hair. That's it. Out of reflex, I was kicked. It couldn't have been because I naïvely stood behind Cody instead of to her side? Or maybe she was an unwilling participant to the beautification process! Whatever reason I was sent soaring through the air smooth as a trapeze artist, we will never know.

Don't use old beater clippers on any animal,

particularly a horse.

Purchase a good pair.

More importantly,

don't stand behind a horse.

Horses kick really hard!

Soft nuzzle rubs are affectionately exchanged. If intent was in her fickle heart, I might feel differently about this love we have going on. I do believe it was an accident.

I choose to continue to love her and let it go

despite the pain she caused.

Now to practice that same love

on others that cause me pain,

It's not so easy to do,

but I must choose.

Friends

Are a rare find

Gems

To cherish

For a lifetime

Investment required

Time allotted

Price to pay

Nothing of value

Comes cheaply

Dividends only come

When the price of time is paid

Misty

9

Misty knows... when I lace up my dusty old Ariats, it's a dead giveaway. Around here, the aroma of dry manure stimulates excitement. I rarely take Misty to the ranch, as she's a royal pain. This dog will herd anything that moves. She makes a nuisance of herself. I guess she can't help it; herding is what shelties are created to do.

"*Can I go? Can I go? Please. Pretty please!*" Misty puts on the maul. "*Oh, please! Please take me with you!*" The beggar persists. "*I won't leave you alone until you say yes!*" She's been trained to beg; "some" in the house think it's cute.

I give way to Misty's relentless pleading routine. Certainly, I can't deprive the poor girl of an opportunity to harass the masses. If she knew how to lasso, she'd be dangerous. "OK, Misty, OK, you can come," wondering if I'll live to regret the hasty decision.

The doorbell rings. Chaos erupts, Misty spins her beefy soul out of control! How she remains so square with all this bizarre twirling, I have no idea. Why she doesn't hyperventilate, get dizzy and fall over, is beyond me. I find this behavior annoying, while others deem it "adorable". Nevertheless, it does add a splash of comedy relief to our otherwise boring lives.

She needs therapy.

My little sister (size two and four years younger) has arrived. She is not as twisted as yours truly. Life circumstances taught both of us to become more flexible. It's a difficult process, but she has adapted. I'd like to think I too have improved. We no longer take ourselves too seriously.

Our plan is to horse around while she's in town.

"Come on, Misty, let's go for a ride!" Enthusiastically she waddles to the door.

Sis and I clamor with anticipation of our first ride together. We grab hats and water bottles, then turn and trip over the silly dog standing in our way. Off to the ranch we go!

Billows plume as we blaze up the dirt road to the ranch. I turn to apologize. I'm afraid with all the horses available, Denise might assume the plan is to bootleg another horse.

"Sorry, Denise, we only one horse to ride. We'll make this work. It'll be fun! Cody is such a hoot, you'll love her."

"I expected nothing less," Denise responds.

"Good, because Cody is all we have."

Denise is always gracious and kind. Can you tell? She's the sweeter of the two of us. Denise is tall and slim with long, dark curly locks. It's obvious we come from the same set of genes. We look alike and laugh at everything whether it's funny or not. A strange family trait that some would deny.

I share how Cody has challenged me, that she keeps me stimulated and stretched both physically and mentally. Not to mention the deep gratification of our relationship.

I warn, "You can expect the unexpected."

Denise reassures me, "Don't worry about me, I ride a cutting horse used in the competition circuit."

"Alrighty then, you'll be an old pro." Who could argue with that kind of experience? She certainly can't be any worse than me.

Excited, we catch up and tell audacious true stories, as we groom Cody and keep an eye on the silly dog. Misty is not your typical petite, adorable sheltie seen in photos. Clunky and awkward better describe the poor soul. Nevertheless, she is on the job, earning her keep, doing what she does best, chasing rabbits and prairie dogs. The serenity of the ranch is under siege. She is so proud.

I quiz Denise while tightening up the cinch of the saddle, "Do you want to ride doubles today, or alone?"

"Doubles sounds fun." Animatedly, she smiles through the giggles. (We're sisters, what can I say.)

"You ride on the back. I need room to accommodate my voluptuous curves."

"That's OK by me." Denise kindly accommodates my need for more seat confinement.

It's hard to find western jeans in a size fourteen or above. Manufacturers discriminate against curvaceous-ness. Do they think only Skinny Minnies enjoy looking good in western threads? Maybe they're compelled to save a horse. Maybe we should revolt and ride naked! I bet after seeing such a sight, manufacturers would be highly compelled to design super-sized western wear.

"Girls, expect the memo in your mailbox to alert you of the 'Big Naked Ride!' coming your direction soon." A complimentary business tip for all designers out there, you are most welcome. Big girls rule! Enough commentary about nakedness, back to our story at hand...

Under normal circumstances, I walk Cody out a bit to expel air and tighten up the cinch. This allows for a tighter and more secure saddle fit. Distracted by funny stories, and prairie dogs herded into holes by an overly excited sheltie. "Normal" is preempted. What a grand day in the life of an old dog that typically has nothing to do but lounge.

Smart pets need a job

to encourage self-worth

and keep out of trouble.

You know, like children.

"Come on, Misty, we're going for a ride, leave the critters alone!" She never pays attention to the sound of my voice. I shout loader, "MISTY! COME ON!"

Reluctantly she obeys, shifts her attention from herding small animals to nipping the heels of large ones. We shake our heads and roll our eyes at her obnoxious uncontrollable behavior.

"She'll kick you, Misty, leave Cody alone!" Instructions fall on deaf ears. She continues to nip. "**Now stop it!**" I reprimand! The last thing we need is for this silly dog to be hurt.

You know the mount routine by now, left leg up, place in the stirrup and throw the right leg over the saddle. We giggle as I hoist Denise behind the saddle skirt. We're off! We travel only a short distance before Cody suddenly stops. I see the trouble.

"Mercy, Cody! Are you still buffaloed by a ditch?"

Rhythmically we rock! That's right; back and forth we rock before lunging like a deer!

"Yee-haw!" Shouts of laughter burst forth.

"Yip, yip, yip!"

"OH, GREAT!" I snarl at Misty. "I knew she'd be more trouble than fun," under my breathe I mutter.

Misty neurotically barks on the other side of the ditch. She can't figure how to crossover. Slightly irritated, I dismount; pick up the dog, leap over the trench and start all over again.

"OK," I growl, "Are we ready now?"

"We're ready," Denise acknowledges with glee.

"Grab the saddle's edge and hold on!"

With a slight squeeze to Cody's belly, we're off. A brisk walk quickly transitions with a click of the tongue to a gallop. Herding Cody seems to be Misty's latest passion. Maybe we can shake off this annoyance. Only wishful thinking, what a pest she is.

Sometimes we just don't know when

to back off, do we?

I'm not so sure I know either.

Leisurely, we ride to higher ground and revel in the smog-free, unobstructed views. Today is crystal-clear, unlike where Denise lives near San Diego. We can see the spectacular Flatirons near Boulder. Pikes Peak pokes through the clouds to the south. It's that purple mountains' majesty thing goin' on. You know, that part in the song, "America the Beautiful" where emerald mountains glisten with stunning shades of purples and plums. Gorgeous ... Spectacular ... Indescribable ... WOW! There is no place as serene and magnificent as the Colorado Rockies.

This is pretty much an uneventful ride, other than the obnoxious dog who has acquired a sinful taste for heel nipping. Our consistent chatter abruptly stops with a calm whisper from behind the saddle, "Let's get out of here."

"Why?"

"There are coyotes out here."

"Are you serious?" I balk, looking around.

"Where?"

Denise cautions, "Look along the ridge."

My eyes survey the hill. Sure enough, not just one coyote, either. Rather, several, six to eight of them. I do believe that is commonly referred to as a pack! Vicious coyotes have strategically encircled us.

"Yikes! Let's get out of here before we become dinner!"

Cody on the brunt end of a good squeeze. Fight or flight kicks into gear! A heated battle breaks out between a dog relentlessly chomping at horse hooves and our panicked attempt to escape the pack of coyotes.

"MISTY, STOP IT! LEAVE US ALONE!" Hooves fly. I visualize Misty in flight, too! That is, if she doesn't get out of the way!

"MISTY, STOP IT!" I scold.

Coyotes hold their ground. Nervous fear oozes from my pores as the pack grows. Our safety is in serious jeopardy! Possibly our very lives!

To escape a coyote attack, one must put the spurs to the ol' mare! Now add a cantankerous saddle! We gallop as fast as Cody's little legs will carry two riders, while I attempt to reposition the slippery lop-eared saddle, Denise clings for dear life!

"O-O-O-O-O-O, yikes!" the voice of despair cries from the rear. Denise tightly grips the cantle for the petrifying descent.

Despite her awkward position, she keeps me abreast of the coyotes' whereabouts. The pack zeros in on the hoof-nipper. City girls in a dog fight of a different sort. A dog at our heels, a rolling saddle, and under siege by a pack of coyotes! What a sight we must be!

Out of the blue, a loud whistle comes from the barn. Again, we hear the whistle. This time Misty darts toward the corral. To our relief, she is off our tail and out of danger!

On the other hand, under our saddle is a spirited mare galloping down a very steep hill, which, seems steeper than ever before. The same hill Cody learned to fly on; that hill. Peppered with rocks... A serious amount of rocks. The kind that cause head injuries... Yes, those kinds of rocks, coupled with being under attack by coyotes, and a saddle with a mind of its own. A recipe for disaster, a D E A D L Y combination!

"S-T-O-P, I'm falling off!!" Denise frantically cries while dangling off the saddle at a 45-degree angle. Or so it seemed.

Options race through my mind as lightning. Choices present themselves. Attacked and devoured by coyotes?

Head injuries? Fatalities? Physically fight off the enemy? I don't own a pistol. I have no club. Thank goodness, I'm wearing my kick-ass boots! OK, I'll take chances with vicious wildlife and stop!

"Whoa, girl, whoa!" I pull heavy on the reins.

Over the rocks we stumble as the decent begins to slow. **"Whoa, Cody!"** More aggressively I pull on the reins! Down the rock-infested hillside we charge until Cody is overcome with a bit of reason. The race abruptly ends. Stop happens. Traumatized bodies roll to the ground. Denise doesn't have far to go.

I have no idea how I remained upright. Maybe I wasn't. The saddle was practically under Cody's belly. Just maybe, I was falling off, too. Denise says I was. But this is my story and I'll tell it the way I remember! OK, just maybe, I did slip horizontally! What does upright look like anyway?

Both of us burst into hysterical snorting and laughter! That laughing in the face of danger, is hereditary. What can I say? We just can't help ourselves; it's what we do. After all, it was funny and we're sisters! Bent over busting a gut, we cannot contain ourselves. For the next several minutes we remain in our happy place of uncontrollable hysteria.

We regain composure (somewhat) and tighten up my frothy mare's saddle. Legs and presence of mind are rattled and shaken, only my warped sense of humor remains intact. Smitten with amnesia, the coyote worry fades away. To mount Cody with noodle legs is entirely too much effort. Bow leggedness reminds us just how great it is to ride a horse. Traversing the hill, we quiver, horse in tow close behind. I glance over the ridge; the frenzy has evaporated!

This was enough fun for one day's adventure!

Misty hangs with Boots at the corral. Boots noticed the pack of coyotes and whistled for the crazy dog. "Those coyotes were after your dog, not you or the horse." Boots smirks, "Coyotes don't eat humans."

"Oh, OK, we were not knowing." Our eyes lock and hilarious snorting erupts once again! We're sisters, what can I say?

Boots must have seen the whole thing. I'm sure he got a big charge out of us city slicker wannabes.

For a safe adventure

tighten up your saddle and hang on!

Life is full of surprises!

Enjoy the ride

And while you're at it

learn to laugh at yourself!

Oh, and keep watch on

small barking dogs,

they are no match for coyotes.

Sunshine and Sunny overlooking city of Golden, CO

Floozy

10

Cody is a National Show horse, a mix of two breeds. Her Arabian oozes in the prance. See the graceful way she carries her swan arched neck and small framed face. Not to mention the proud gait and quick step. On-the-other-hand, the Saddlebred, bloodline is well-known for their presence and style, thus tagged the "peacock". She knows it too! Watch her strut! A captivating wonder, isn't she? You can't help but admire such poise and beauty. Cody lives up to it, in spades! Not certain if this breed is known to be super intelligent or just exquisite to look at.

Today, my Show Horse has a sense of knowing this is no ordinary day. Rarely does she look back, glancing at her peers left in their personal accommodations. Generally, she could care less.

"Hey, guys, my girl is taking me places. I'm leavin' this playpen behind. Catch y'all later."

Cody doesn't know it yet, but the next several days are consumed with all things of importance besides my beloved horse. Thus, "RELEASE" is the word of the week.

Jostling for position to open the gate. A power struggle of sorts between beast and her human. The narrow path of freedom awaits. I unbuckle and remove her headstall before Cody anxiously plows over me, ever so graceful, of course. Seasoned with tenacity and a pinch of attitude, the gate flings wide open! Cody quickly disappears. A cloud of dust follows dancing hooves celebrated by a series of joyful quick bucks. Grateful oozes as her twisted body contorts with theatrical flair. She's off to introduce herself to the new kids on the block, Bruno and Coco, recent additions to the pasture. The herd has alienated the newcomers, as if untouchables, lepers, outcasts.

I guess I'm naïve as to the pecking order process in the animal kingdom. It seems so cruel and senseless. Why can't the other horses accept these two?

What do I know? I only know what I see.

Are we to study wildlife

so we don't duplicate the same behavior?

Are the lessons to be learned

on how NOT to behave?

Thoughts to ponder.

Bruno is a tall, lean Quarter Horse, coffee in color. He's nothing to write home about. Coco, on the other hand, is a spotted, gray Appaloosa who thinks she's a Paint, acting so pretty and proud, but she's not.

Sometimes we too think we're all that...

but we're not.

It's a hard pill to swallow, I know.

The welcoming committee warmly greets Cody. I'm intrigued to watch the ritualistic acceptance dance transpire. Tension fills the air as nostrils flare. Horses check each other out. Do you see it? Can you sense it? Heads shoot straight up! Necks stiffen. Snorts intimidate. It's an all-out full alert! Ears point forward. Now agitated, they flatten to the backside. Thick lips wrinkle a goofy grin. Grass-stained teeth give aggressive nips. I'm not certain if this validates who bites harder or what. Suddenly, all horses retreat, I speculate for fear of retaliation from their opponent. Hostility is replaced with gentle sniffs, of each-other's noses, necks and rear-ends. Heads lower to a more natural position. The dominant game has concluded.

"Welcome!"

Acceptance has come.

"Whew, what an ordeal!"

The three new confidants run off together to take on the herd. As if the other horses are any match for these misfits.

People do the same thing, this herding process.

Acceptance or rejection

with a mere raising of the nose

we size each other up and determine

if you're a friend or foe.

Generally, we don't bother with

rear end inspections.

Or do we?

I'm confident Cody will not receive a thrashing over the next several days. Hear tell, that's how horses establish dominance. With a simple farewell I bid, "Have fun, Cody!"

You don't throw your horse out

in the pasture with unknown horses.

WATCH THEM get acquainted.

You know,

like you do with your own children.

Don't leave them with strangers.

Think safety first!

Seven days later...

Today's challenge is to locate Cody, and reel her back in. The last time I searched this massive prairie was during a downpour. I trudged through the muddy pasture in a trench coat, wiping the rain as it cascaded from my hat's brim. It was one of those chilling days when curling up by a cozy fire with a novel would have been the more sensible thing to do. Instead, I was out saving my horse from a thunderstorm. As if she is not waterproof! Today, I'll swelter under the same trench coat, but will not get soaked. Off to the tack shack, I grab the lead rope and royal purple head stall, lace it over my shoulder and under my arm. Retrieve the dented Folgers coffee can filled with grain and head into the desolate abyss in hopes of a speedy horse recovery.

"CODY, CODY!" I call into the thin air, "COME HERE, GIRL," hoping she'll respond to the sound of my pleasant call. That's part of that bonding thing, right? They know and respond to your voice out of love and admiration, like our children do. We've been partners long enough. By now, I expect her total devotion and cooperation. Yeah, right!

Horses have a great sense of hearing. As loud as my voice is, I'm almost certain it will not carry over twelve hundred acres of wilderness. This mare can be anywhere. On the edge of the pasture, I scan the land. I see absolutely no evidence of horses. None.

"Cody!" I shout, rattling the can of manipulation. Oops, you can't hear a full can rattle. Now I'm stuck carrying a five-pound dead weight.

I begin the hilly hike, admiring impressive views off in the distance. "CODY!" I shout, while engrossed in the sight of beautiful rosy tilted rocks. The Flatirons direct aliens to the most "intriguing" humanoids on earth. No, I'm not talking Hollywood. I'm talking Boulder, a strange collection of creative types. Where affluence, college students, hippies from a by-gone era, coexists with free-thinkers and tree huggers. Now sprinkle on a serious dose of quirkiness, and you have Boulder!

I press on. If I shout out, "LET'S RIDE, GIRL!" will a voice ricochet back a song? Listen. Do you hear it? Bummer. I don't either. Where is she? If Cody can't hear me, I'm forced to search this entire dry, desolate range on foot! I'm not the least bit happy. In fact, I'm a little peeved. I scout over the rolling hills. I should have brought water and packed a lunch.

In high altitude (mile high),

water is a necessity.

Carry it as you do your phone,

it could save your life.

It hasn't rained in months. Dust clings to parched boots

in search of moisture. I guard my footing to avoid a twisted ankle on this rock-infested prairie, as I conquer each hill in hopes to catch a glimpse of the herd. Instead, there is nothing but more hills. Where is she? Am I delusional or have they all vanished? That's impossible! The silent coffee can shakes, my butt sags, and the lasso rope drags as I wrestle it slipping from my shoulder.

The sun tips towards the cloud covered mountains. Flirting with a hunt-a-thon, recovery is nowhere in sight. Weary of eating dirt clods, dehydrated as a withering leaf, in hopes of stumbling upon a waterin' hole over the next ridge. I will not be deterred. My feet are sore and ache beyond imagination. Press on. Don't give up hope, I whine.

"There you are! Well, you big rascal, I found you! No wonder you didn't respond!"

Skip and Cody are nestled together, looking pretty cozy and friendly. Lashes bat discreetly as if to say, *"Can't you see, I have found love? Why do you display such hostility towards me?"*

"Did I interrupt you, Cody?" I lasso her with a scold. "I've been looking for you everywhere! Sorry, Skip, it's time for her to go home."

Horse in tow, we head to the barn. You ask, why don't you just jump on her and ride back? Sounds like a great idea, I wish I could. But I'm not limber enough to mount a horse's back without a means to pull myself up. Yes, I know my riding skills have improved, but not to that level! Cody doesn't come equipped with a ladder, saddle or hoist on her back. There are plenty of rocks in the pasture, but none large enough to help me mount. Maybe it's the lack of athleticism, not riding skill, if truth be told.

Like a race car we sputter on fumes toward the pit. I glance back to see what the holdup is. To my amusement, we have us an awkward piggyback situation. No wonder the lack of cooperation.

"Skip! Get off her!" on heedless ears my command falls. I impatiently wait. "Are you done yet?"

Cody's full attention is required to safely pass over the barbed wire fence hovering near my feet. They finish their business. Cody steps over the rusty wire without mishap. Greatly disturbed by his lover's departure, yet unwilling to leave his domain, Skip nickers anxiously. The further we roam, the louder he neighs, announcing to the world, **"She's mine now, not yours! Don't take my babe, bring her back. Bring Cody back, I tell you!"**

"Whatever, Skip."

"I love you, Cody, darling!" he wails.

We arrive at the stall. My shoulder is cognizant of playing tug of war with a horse and rope. "What is the hold-up, now!?" I snap and abruptly turn around, only to find Cody's rump in the face of Shirley's old gray mare. With a stiff tug on the rope, we saunter to the next horse. Admirers line up at the rail. Cody stops and puts her rear in the gelding's face.

Proud as a peacock, she announces, *"See what I've been up to. I've been with Skip, the big guy in the pasture. Check it out! We had a really good time! He's mine, we're hooked up."*

We continue to share the good news as we pass each stall. I can hardly believe the outrageous encounter.

My observation of this incredible experience

makes me realize

hormones, people and horses

have a lot of similarities.

Bragging rights are her crown of glory; Cody proudly enters her pen as queen for the day, smiling and content.

All in a day's play.

Cody covered in frost

Broken Heart

11

Bruno and Coco love Cody. I mean they LOVE Cody! You'll see the two of them huddle close by, as if to say,

"Hey! You, over there!"

"Me?"

"Yeah, you! We want to play with Cody!"

On numerous occasions, they frolic together while I muck the stall. That's a delicate way of saying, I shovel manure. The three have developed quite the relationship. The trio never mingles with the rest of the herd. It's us against them.

One blistering hot summer day, I release Cody into the pasture. It isn't what I see that is so strange; it is what I don't see.

Bruno is absent.

To rid the stall of manure doesn't take long on a hot dry day, as horse turds turn into flour dust.

Shirley and I visit a spell before inquiring minds ask about Bruno's whereabouts. "Ask Boot's, he'll know."

"Hey, Boots, where's Bruno? I don't see him in the pasture."

Shaking his head, Boots solemnly responds, "He died a couple of days ago."

Shock pierces my heart. "Died?! Oh my!" Tears swell, and my gut tightens into a knot, "I am so sorry!" I choke back. "How awful!"

"Yeah, we found him dead out in the pasture." Boots lowers his head. "Paula is really torn up over the loss. She's had those horses over ten years."

Dread and sorrow fill my heart as I give condolences. I feel sad for both Paula and Coco. What a traumatic experience to go through. I can't imagine their pain.

Heavy-hearted, I grab the lead rope and grain can, then head to the pasture on retrieval mission. Once again, I hunt everywhere for Cody. The pasture is divided by barbed wire and rickety wooden posts. Passing through several gates, I finally spot Cody hanging out with Coco, hovering close to the herd.

"Here you are." I fasten the lead rope to her headstall. "Come on, Cody, it's time to return to where you belong."

Coco tags close as a needy toddler not wanting to leave her mom. *"I'm coming with you."*

We approach the gate at the upper pasture. "Sorry, Coco, Cody's coming with me. She can play again some other time."

It's a challenge, but I manage to squeeze Cody through

the fence opening without Coco thrusting her way from the other side. Extremely upset, Coco franticly paces back and forth, clobbering anything in sight. Coco's outcry breaks my heart. Her gut-wrenching nicker is relentless.

"PLEASE TAKE ME WITH YOU," Coco whinnies from the deepest depths of her soul and might.

Our friends cry out for us,

inaudibly at times.

When they do,

give them the support they need.

Someday

you might need the same.

I can't bear it. I turn back to watch Coco wildly pacing in desperation, endeavoring to jump the fence. The heart-wrenching scene is extremely disturbing.

Coco is working into a lathered frenzy; she'd better settle down. The thought occurs to me, she's going to die of a broken heart. It truly is breaking mine to watch her bellow out in desperation for her only friend left in the entire world.

Why the thought never occurred to match the two horses together, I'll never know. Slowly Cody and I make our way back to the stall to tuck her in for the evening.

Pondering over Bruno's death and the effect Cody's departure had on Coco, I'm deeply troubled over the event I witnessed.

Several days pass. I return to ride. Cody is released in the corral while I muck the stall. Chores completed in a snap and when I return, I stumble upon a most peculiar scene. Cody's passion and desire to join the herd is noticeably missing. She just stands there, staring over the fence.

"What's wrong, girl?" knowing something's not right. I look out over the ranch, trying to see what she sees. It isn't what we see; it's what we don't see. Coco is nowhere in sight. Usually she is close by, ready to play. We don't see her anywhere.

Determined to find answers, I go on the hunt. "Hey! Marvin, where is Coco?"

"Coco died this week," he disclosed.

"NO! NOT COCO, TOO!"

"Yeah, it's pretty sad, huh?"

"What did she die of?" I inquire.

The medical term he used was more of that equinese, leaving me totally clueless.

"What is that?" curiosity bellows out.

Shaking his head, he sadly responds, "A broken heart."

My own heart sinks as I quietly relinquish a deep sigh of anguish. I knew it! A broken heart! I'm the one who took Cody away from Coco. I triggered this horrible tragedy. Her only friend left in the world. The separation anxiety was more than the mare could bear. I walk away, grief-stricken, heartbroken and tears streaming down my cheeks.

Horses have a tremendous ability

to love, suffer pain

and sense deep loss.

Every bit as much as people do.

Maybe more.

Home on the Range

12

ATVs squeal like pigs in the pasture. What's going on? The deafening sound of four-wheelers is highly unusual here on the ranch.

"Hey, what's happening, Boots?"

"We have a new calf! He just got shots."

This city girl is totally in the dark why shots are administered to a newborn calf. Curiosity kicks in. "What's that all about?"

"Steroids." Boots pours much-needed education into this clueless city girl's soul. "Each calf receives steroids after they're born. It'll put eighty pounds on a head of beef over the course of its lifetime. If anything happens to the calf before it turns four months of age, it must be destroyed. You can't eat the meat."

"Really?"

"Yes, ma'am, the meat's no good, we burn the calf, if it dies."

"Burn it!?"

"Yes, ma'am, we have a special incinerator built to burn up livestock here on the ranch." Boots gives clueless the lowdown on ranch life not revealed on the earlier tour. Maybe Shirley is unaware, or just preferred not to disclose the graphic details.

"Eighty pounds, huh? That's a lot."

This conversation kicks my instinctive brainiac side into motion. If steroids put eighty pounds on a calf and we digest it into our bodies, what does it do to us?

"Do you think that's why young girls develop breasts at such an early age?" I question Boots.

"I'm pretty sure it is." He nods emphatically. "No, I'm certain of it."

"Wow! Hmm... Well, I've got to go; see you later, Boots." While I shovel manure, I mull the thought-provoking conversation in relation to our nation's epic rise of obesity. Is this a contributor?

Could steroids in our food

be the culprit for the obesity epidemic?

If it's poisonous

> *to the meat of the calf now,*
> *what is it to us later?*

The penalties or benefits of "progress" are revealed much later, if at all. That's what camouflage is for, isn't it, to conceal what we don't want exposed? Our mistakes, for example? Then, of course, we can place the blame on everything but where it belongs. Humanoids are masters of disguise.

> *The high price we pay*
>
> *keeping our heads buried in profit.*

Huh, that's a lesson I never saw coming. Given time to reflect, this thinking process can get pretty scary. I don't claim to know if my conclusions are true or accurate. I only know these are my thoughts on the matter based on heightened awareness and our conversation.

Later the same summer ~

Yet another greenhorn encounter at the ranch.

My unquenchable curiosity is aroused once again by the hubbub at the stalls. Several rancher types are spotted hovering around Boots' horse, Red, who is generally found grazing in the pasture. That isolated stall is always empty, but today Red consumes many sets of eyes. Of course, I can't leave the commotion alone. What I see is pretty gruesome. Let's listen in as Boots and his father discuss what happened.

"See these marks across his chest?" Marvin points to foot-long slashes of flesh dangling from the horse's chest.

"He and a bear must have really gotten into it. He put up a good fight." Boots evaluates the horse. "Judging by the multiple swipes, Red fought for his life."

"Judging by this deep gouge," fingers and fist cover his raw chest area, "the bear must have chased Red into a fence post."

Red's entire chest flesh lays open. The men measure and discuss the gruesome hole the size of a basketball. A man's fist can slide into the cavity. I see no blood, only the woven tapestry of ripped muscle and missing hair.

"It'll heal up quickly." Marvin encourages. "We'll just have to wait to see if the gelding is usable." The evaluation concludes as the men begin to break away.

But wait! I want to know more...

"Bear, what are you talking about?"

"Do you smell that offensive odor?" Boots asks.

Only on occasion does my nose work. But, this odor is so distinct it cannot be avoided, even for these ineffective nostrils. Both brows rise and eyes spring wide, I respond with an insistent nod.

"That is bear!

They stink to high heaven.

That's how you distinguish what it is,

by the foulness in the air."

Most of us city dwellers have never smelled anything close to it. Nor do you really want to. It is indescribable. My best wild stab of description is the foulest, nastiest kitchen. Can you smell the refrigerator? The food remains, yet it's been shut off, for a very long time. That kind of foul!

"Wow! Boots, do you think it's safe to ride in the pasture today?"

"You might want to use the arena. You can see what happened to this poor old guy."

~~~~

I didn't hear the outcome of Red before we left to board elsewhere. What a wild experience it was. An education of a lifetime was acquired at home on the range.

Life in the country is often misunderstood.

Is it because of the sharp contrast

with urban life?

We've gotten so concerned about receiving

Credentialed education,

We place little value on experience.

What does it take to merge

practical application

with "book learned" knowledge?

Parents,

Teachers can't do it all.

Expose your kids to life's diversities.

There are a lot of exciting opportunities

to explore!

ST

Big Move

13

Yahoo! Today is moving day. "Say goodbye to apartment living, Cody."

Stan and Connie offered to exchange hair services for boarding. This arrangement will save me a ton of money, not to mention Cody can stretch her legs, kick up her heels and run like the wind on two acres of three-foot-tall grass. Ah, to freely graze... A charming, rusty old barn, a small corral enclosed by an old weathered fence, right out of a storybook! Who could ask for anything more?

My compadres are transplants from Texas. Stan is a confident, short, muscular guy just a few years older than I. His considerably younger adoring wife, Connie, is a hard-working machine. Even after ten years in Colorado, they continue to speak Texan. That's a combination of a slight drawl and odd sayings, like, "In a pig's eye." Now what sense does that make and what does it mean? I don't get it. One might think they were "foreigners".

Here's the plan. I'll saddle up and ride. It's dirt roads all the way. The only town to pass through is Leyden. Ben's job is to load up the tack and follow. We should be at the barn in a few hours.

Not having a horse trailer might seem inconvenient to some; I choose to see it as an opportunity for adventure.

Life is all about the journey.

One might ask, "Why don't you borrow a horse trailer for the move?" I'd have to say, "Easy peasy...and miss out on all kinds of fun? Why?"

"Cody, this is it. We're moving today, girlfriend. It'll be great! We have a long way to go. We can do this. I believe in you girl." This is my first pure endurance ride. It's only two and a half miles.

Check out our wagon train, the bed overflows with tack supplies. Inside sits my smokin' husband, and I don't mean "hot"! Ben nurses his cold morning's coffee mug while filling the cab with stale pungent cigarette smoke. He tells me he's trying to quit. A story I've heard for years.

Tucked away in trusty saddlebags are a few provisions. Give exploration the spurs! You know, scout the terrain, and watch for rattlers, coyotes and traffic. All supplies are loaded up and so am I. "Cody, say goodbye to your old friends! Green pastures, here we come!" With that said, I reach down in assurance to lovingly pat her strong, arched neck, "Let's spy out the land."

"Wagons, HO!" With a click of my tongue, I wave to move the herd forward, like an ol' wagon master.

Humor me for a moment. Step back in time. Imagine loved ones line the dirt drive to see us off. This ol' cowgirl gestures sweet goodbyes. It's a bittersweet conclusion to our time spent here on the ranch. Even the horses in the pasture sense change in the wind. Skip whinnies relentlessly off in the distance.

A deep inhale then exhale shudders the saddle beneath as Cody soulful whinnies in reply, *"I will miss you terribly Skip! I love you."*

I attempt to soothe her fears and concerns with a soft, tender stroke to her neck, "You'll be OK, girl."

Straight ahead, the intimidating highway awaits. Traffic races over the hill. The road is barely crossed by car safely, much less by horse. The cross junction is impaired by hilly terrain. You could say, I'm extremely nervous about making it to the other side. I trust Cody will listen and move with speed to avoid being splattered on the road. We have more confidence in each other by now, yet I still expect the unexpected.

Uneasy, we begin the dangerous crossing! Here it goes. Take a deep breath. Not anxious to jump out in fifty mile an hour traffic, I glance both directions and wait. Watch for the big break. A firm squeeze applied to Cody's ribcage, followed by a swift kick to her belly! We have no time to quarrel about what to do or who's in charge. This is do or die! Here goes! Quickly, we trot across Highway 93.

"Whew!!" What a relief. "Good job, Cody! Well done, girl! I'm so proud of you."

Thankful to be alive! This is our first time to ride away from the ranch by ourselves! Basking in gratefulness, we rose to the challenge! "YA-HOO!"

A short jaunt down the road, my grand wagon train illusions diminish. A power struggle emerges from down under. Cody's heart wants to turn around. Mine, on the other hand, is set on proceeding eastward.

"There is freedom in the east, tall fertile grass, two acres to roam, no more pent-up stall for you, girl! Not to mention, free room and board!"

Retaliation prevention plan is implemented with a quick dismount. Cody is pleased to walk alongside a companion. Happy knees, happy horse, happy life. Calmly, caressing my needy mare's neck, hoping to reinforce benefits of her new home. She's not buying it; Cody is totally unimpressed. The further from the ranch we travel, the slower the pace. I grow weary with the lack of enthusiasm. Hooves shuffle the path of resistance.

"Cody, we don't have all day!" Impatiently I chastise. I've had it with obstinate! I swing my leg up and over the saddle to mount her once again. Firm instructions make an obvious impact; Cody picks up the pace for a short distance but then, a revolt happens! Desiring the familiar, this stubborn mare attempts to turn around. A fight erupts.

Slightly perturbed, I do my best to remind Cody, "**I am the master. You are the horse.** You do what I say, not the other way around! **Let's go!**" My patience wears thin.

Fighting slows down progress.

Jockeying for position will arise.

When you're the one in charge,

hold your ground!

Two hours pass, and we still haven't reached Leyden. The town is only a short ten-minute jaunt from the ranch. We are exasperated with each other.

"Fine, just fine."

Multiple mental health days are in my future. Are my expectations totally unrealistic? Will miles turn into endless days?

A good wagon master is always prepared

for all types of delay or catastrophe.

Water, food and a sleeping bag

are great items to have on hand.

"THERE WILL BE NO OVERNIGHT CAMPING!" Spurs would be a good tool about now, if you know what I mean. Although annoyed, I choose words of encouragement. "Come on, Cody. We're headed to greener pastures where you can kick up your heels, run, play and graze on fresh, tall grass. You won't be cooped up all day. It'll be grand! I promise, you'll love it!" I continue my powerful bribery motivation speech. Should a discussion on the topic of bribery carry any weight! My words fall on deaf ears. She balks.

You never know unless you try!

What a struggle! FINALLY, after fighting all morning, we mosey upon our half-way point. I relish the benchmark of Leyden.

Life in the Old West just stepped off the pages of a storybook. Children are playing in the streets of this quaint, rural town. There might be a population of sixty if you include their pets. Traffic is minimal, no streetlights or stop signs. What a charming, weathered, white-picket-fence community. Narrow dirt roads and no sidewalks, that kind of small town. What a moment to savor! A lovely occasion to do a little victory jig!

Only my idea of a victory jig and Cody's idea are distinctly different! This cherished moment of enchantment spoiled by plans of her own. Mutiny! That's right! This mare elevates her style of balking to an entirely new level.

"If you won't turn around then I will!" With fortitude, in the heart of town, my insubordinate mare makes an about-face, completing a quarter turn in the middle of the road! A downright brawl breaks out! It gets real ugly, I tell you! Previously the street was devoid of traffic, that is, until now! Like a magnet, trouble pulls everyone in close. Cars and children screech to a dead stop, not to miss the action. How exciting for this small town! An afternoon honest to goodness duke-out! A duel of sorts. A war of brute strength, willpower and courage. That's right, horse and rider tangle for position on the streets of Leyden!

Enforcing the eastward plan with a strong rein and stern kick to her belly's right side, I'll show this mare who's boss!

With plans of her own, Cody informs me, *"West is the direction I'm going!"* Before I know it, the discussion is elevated to HI-HO, Silver heights! A scary Lone Ranger pose, reaching for the heavenlies moment. This only makes sense if you are old enough to know the children's TV show. Trust me; rearing up on two hind legs, never looked so scary! All eyes are fixed on us. You'd think the circus was in town.

Weight heavy in the stirrups; heels are down, I remain planted in the saddle, battling for every inch! Believe it or not, completely in control, no matter how it appears! Well, that is other than being straight up in the air. But for that extraordinary moment frozen in time, I'm totally in control! What an unbelievable experience!

Ride 'em, cowgirl! I'm so proud of myself. Kudos to me! Mercy, how your riding skills have improved, girlfriend!

Cody quickly finds solid ground under all four hooves. Passionately a firm hand lands smack on her neck! **"Cody, you are going where I tell you! We're not turning back! Do you hear me?"**

Suddenly, I clearly hear the Spirit of God speak.

"My kids are just like that!

They balk at me as well

And put Me to the test.

I try to lead them to greener pastures

But they think I don't know what's best.

Not wanting to leave their friends

And experience something new.

Yes, they balk at me too."

Ouch. I too am like Cody at times.

Half-heartedly, Cody submits to my lead. She's not happy about it. Just to make her point, she remains in slow gear the entire journey.

I'm miserable. My thighs are sore, my shins scream, my butt is paralyzed and bears the shape of a leather saddle. I'm both chafed and frosted!

Sunset is upon us. To stop for the evening is not in the cards. This wagon master has no lantern. I dread the idea of being on Indiana Street in the dark, hidden by all the blind rolling hills. The only lights on the road are on Ben's truck bringing up the rear.

"Let's move it, Cody!"

I'm tired of dragging butt and wrestling all day with an obstinate mare. She has worn me to a frazzle. It's time to go home. Adventure and persistence, attitude and balk just melt into an agonizing blend.

The lovely sunset has gone unnoticed. We are beyond the

horizon turned dark. Magnificent stars glisten against the night sky. Oncoming head lights occasionally break up the darkness, lighting our path. Past hungry, I'm utterly exhausted as I drag my weary soul slowly up Stan and Connie's drive, just before midnight.

The tripled in weight saddle slides off a tired horse. Not a word spoken, Ben and I unload all the equipment by the dimly lit yard lamp. We climb into the silent truck and I mutter, "Let's go home."

Mission accomplished.

"Brat!"

Greener Pastures

Why do we resist you so?

Do we not believe you are here to stay?

Do we resist dreaming

For fear of failure?

So what if we fail?

Is that so horrible?

People will laugh at me

You say.

So what if they do!

No matter who

Or what you are

Is comfort more desirable than regret?

Maybe the irony of

Elusive green pastures

Is not attempting to find them at all.

Protection

14

Stop signs, double yellow lines, paying taxes, no weapons in the classroom, are life's simpler rules for our safety. Most comply for the sole purpose of maintaining order. When one chooses not to act in accordance with the rules, their behavior painfully affects others. Our entire world is established on the premise of safeguarding each other's well-being. It prevents chaos. Protection is an odd fellow, with which we have a love-hate relationship. Unless we are somewhat demented, we want protection and maybe even feel entitled to it. Most parents are over-protective of their children these days. Understandably so. We want nothing to happen to our kids and try to do everything in our power to equip them for both survival and success.

Plainly said, rules and laws are meant to protect us. We love the safety part. It's the compliance part we take issue with. We all squawk, you can admit it. You don't like being told what to do. Neither do I. Who does?

I'm sure by now you must be wondering what this has to do with Cody? Nothing really. What it does have to do with is the dream I had last night. God frequently speaks to me in dreams, as I believe He does many people. You will see, Cody is instrumental in the explanation of the profound dream.

WARNING!

At this point I must forewarn you:

The content of this chapter

Is controversial

And

of a religious nature!

It may cause blood pressure to rise,

Tempers to flare

Or

Books to hurl through the air!

If you are a candidate for the above,

Skip this chapter.

On the other hand, if you enjoy a good spurrin' of the thought-provoking nature, you might really appreciate this chapter. Are you annoyed by topics of religion? If so, I suggest you move to the next story. If you like what you've read so far, you certainly will enjoy the rest of the book, with less irritation.

I've been teaching adult Sunday school at a small non-denominational church. I'm accustomed to not using any published materials. Instead, I wait on God to give me the lesson. Generally, I receive the Word during the week for the upcoming Sunday. I don't plan it, but opportunity to practice always follows. What good are spiritual matters of life if they aren't also practical?

The core principles we live by

impact everything we do and who we are.

Life is fun! Horses, for example, combine pleasure with practicality. Go figure! God knows me so well.

I'm off to bed with no lesson to teach in the morning. This is a first. I never wait til the last minute. To say the heat is on is a slight understatement!

I awaken early from a dream. The dream is the Sunday school lesson! I only have a short time to prepare. Too late for any application much less, understanding.

I trust God's timing is perfect.

Even if I don't like or understand it.

Ok, here it is, the entire message as it came to me in a dream last night. Including the title: *"There is Protection in Submission."*

What does that mean? Women in particular don't like to hear this! I'm not any different. If you struggle with the Bible being relevant for today, think again. No matter what century we live in, practical principles are woven throughout the good book.

The examples given in the night to explain protection in submission were Jonah, Mary and Jesus. In my dream, God went on to explain,

"This applies to all authority,

a boss, government, husband, teacher.

Even if they are wrong,

there is still protection

FOR YOU,

IF,

you come under their authority.

I dreamt everything except the understanding. This was my dream, like it or not. I know this concept is not well received by a lot of people. I don't care for it much myself. Oddly enough, the Father doesn't consult me nor ask my advice, or my opinion. Resistance is futile.

If you are of the male persuasion, you might not see the impact or if you live in a state of denial, this principle could easily slip past you. Don't allow that to happen! Since you've come this far, stop, think and listen to what is presented.

Jonah:

Jonah was sent by God on a mission. Travel to the town of Nineveh, tell the people to stop their corrupt, sinful behavior! Jonah didn't care much for the assignment so in defiance ran, in hopes to escape the call. Why did Jonah think he had an option?

We are all born

for something bigger than ourselves.

As the story goes, Jonah jumped onboard a ship to save his own skin and avoid God. The ship's destination was the opposite direction of Nineveh.

How silly to think

God doesn't know where we are

or what we're up to.

A raging storm overtook the ship at sea. The frightened crew drew straws to determine who was responsible for their violent fate. Drawing straws was the method used long ago to flush out a guilty party. The lot landed on Jonah. He knew it was his fault all along.

We intuitively know

to own up to what we did.

But, for some reason, most won't.

Do our actions challenge

God to flush us out?

"Toss me overboard," Jonah insisted. They did; the storm quickly diminished. But Jonah was not getting off that easy; a giant fish swam by and swallowed him up.

Three days of marination inside the belly of a fish, will cause one to reconsider actions taken. Let's just say, Jonah's heart was tenderized. Once the decision to be obedient was made, the fish promptly vomited the seaweed-saturated Jonah onto dry land, unharmed and protected.

I ask the Lord, "How can that be considered protection? He was devoured by a giant fish." Then I realize Jonah should have become fish dinner, or died at sea; instead, he was protected by a smelly seaweed wrap.

When one is caught in disobedience,

it's rather embarrassing,

sometimes publicly humiliating.

You can read the entire story for yourself in the Book of Jonah. It's a quick four chapters.

Mary:

Mary was chosen by God to become the Christ Child's mother. Willingly, Mary surrendered to the plan, becoming impregnated by the Holy Spirit before she and Joseph were married. According to the law, her fiancé had every right to stone her. Then came the dream. He was told by an angel, that the child Mary was carrying was conceived by the Holy Spirit. Thus, Joseph submitted to the plan and remained engaged, instead of stoning Mary to death as was the era's custom for unwed mothers. Mary was supernaturally protected.[1]

Pay attention to your dreams!

They might illuminate your world.

Jesus:

"But, Lord, Jesus was crucified." I don't get it, "where is the protection in that?" I receive no answer. Contemplation begins.

When Jesus was an small child, his daddy, Joseph, was warned by an angel in a dream, to "flee in the middle of the night" in order to avoid Pharaoh's plot to kill the Messiah.[2] After pondering, "how was he protected?" I'm smitten with an epiphany: There were many attempts to kill Jesus over his lifetime. **Jesus was protected.** The Son of God laid down his life in submission to the plan. It was never taken from him.[3]

Even though I'm told there is protection in submission that does not mean I have the understanding.

Revelation is caught, not taught.

---

[1]Matthew chapter 1:18-25 [2]Matthew chapter 2:12 [3]1John chapter 3:16

After sharing the divine dream with the class, I wrap up with a simple prayer: "Lord, teach us the meaning of protection in submission."

~~~~

I travel to the barn for my customary Sunday afternoon ride feeling a bit unsettled. This morning's message simmers within. A nervous intuition about what today holds floods my mind. By all outward signs it's just another day. Cloudless is the cobalt aromatic sky. Fall explodes with ruddy leaves tussling in the dirt. Crisp luscious temperatures make for a great ride.

Connie follows her path-beaten trail toward the house when she becomes sidetracked by us at the barn and stops by for a visit.

"Where y'all goin' today?"

"Down to the Ralston Creek path; you want to join us? You could ride your bicycle and follow along."

We've done this dangerous thrill many times before! She rides ahead of us on her ten-speed bike. I hold Cody back a safe distance, but at times we are right on her tail. Connie is bound to feel Cody's hot breath on her back. If she ever got tripped up, we'd stomp right over her backside. Not the smartest way to ride, but that's what daredevils with no horse sense do.

"The folks are gatherin' for supper. I can't, maybe another day. Y'all have a good time, ya hear," the screen door slams as Connie returns to her gray bungalow.

In preparation to ride, I stroke the brush gently across Cody's back. Consumed by the thought, what does the dream mean, not just historically, but for this moment in time?

Submission is not one of this fiercely independent woman's finer attributes. Sometimes I apply what I know well. Other times, well, not so much.

A mixed bag of raw emotions and thoughts run through my heart, mind and body. In some ways I know I'm protected, but I have no doubt this is an ordinary pleasure ride. Before departure I mutter a short prayer, "Lord, I'm submitted to you; protect me."

We saunter down the drive toward the street. Cody is not alarmed by traffic, one of the rare things she is not disturbed by.

A month earlier I heard about a horse out of control. It ran into oncoming traffic. The rider was seriously injured, and the horse was killed. What a dreadful, gory accident.

Leaving the barn, we turn left onto Indiana Street. The equestrian park is only a block or two away. Cars race past at an alarming fifty or so miles an hour. Not the safest, but if everyone stays in their assigned lane, mine being the shoulder, all is fine. Sunday's traffic is lighter, which brings comfort.

Signs of a nervous horse are reflected in the raised head and tail, as well as the steady stream of toots. Cody's gait is skittish, and her ears are at full attention. I can't begin to tell you the reason for her antics. Our surroundings appear to be characteristic for a weekend. Maybe she's in season (that time of month). Need I say more?

I stroke her stiff high neck. "Relax, Cody, relax." Nostrils flare with passionate snorts. Classic signs of fear, anxiety and apprehension elevate into a jitterbug. This girl is throwing a hissy fit, a horsy tantrum in living color! And I thought kids look bad throwing a tantrum. Check this out!

Cody emphatically wants to return

to what's familiar.

When adults resist departure from

their comfort zone, poor behavior erupts.

This type of conduct is, well, unbecoming.

Hopelessly she is overpowered by fear. "Cody, what is wrong with you?" I look around to discover the cause. I see nothing out of the ordinary. Those heifers are always there. They are nothing new, I don't get it. There appears to be no reason for alarm.

"Are those big fur balls annoying you?" I tease. "Don't be scared, cows don't eat horses." I caress Cody's dew drenched neck for a dose of reassurance. A wasted meager attempt to comfort. The fitful jive routine of a moody mare is colorful. She is well rehearsed. Cody shifts back and forth, side to side, doing what she does best, scaring the snot out of me!

"Cody, let's face your fear head-on." I dismount "Goofy" to cross the raceway. One-on-one therapy begins to flow from these loose lips. "Those cows are a block away. They can't attack you, they won't hurt you, they won't eat you. It's just that simple. They never have, they never will." It appears Cody has no appreciation for my encouragement. Therapy is not working. It's hard to reason with an unpredictable mare. Agitated I become. "Forget this nonsense!" I cave. "We're done. This therapy session is over, we're riding!"

NOW FOR THE ANTICIPATED DREAM INTERPRETATION AS RELATED TO CODY!

By now, you know the routine, left leg goes into the twisted stirrup. Next, swing right leg over the saddle. WELL SURPRISE, SURPRISE, old tricks revitalized! Abruptly she spins around, bounces upward and bolts. Banished from the saddle, I am! My back slams abruptly to the ground! My head bounces. Eyeglasses disappear into the nearby grass.

Abandoned on the side of the road, I lie there stunned, wind knocked out of me, yet conscious and aware of what just happened. Stretched out, and dazed for what seems several minutes, I promptly pray over my sore, achy traumatized body. "There will be no repercussion, no swelling, no pain, no bruising and no injury."

Suddenly, I'm swarmed by a mob of riders from across the street. Scared and breathy, the entire West Gait Stables now hover overhead. Concerned faces peer over this shaken body lying on her backside. "We saw a saddled horse run down Indiana with no rider!" Outstretched arms pull me to my feet. "Are you OK?" they quiz in unison.

"I'm OK, but I've lost my glasses." I shake dirt from my hair; having narrowly escaped death, I'm over-whelmed and dazed, but unharmed.

The troupe hunts through the tall-grass in search of missing glasses. As we know, it's difficult to find a needle in a haystack. Reality strikes and eyeglasses are no longer a priority. What about my horse? "Where is she?" Fear grips my heart and tears stream down my cheeks.

"We don't see her anywhere."

I tearfully wail out, "Where is she?"

A stranger hands a familiar pair of twisted glasses. I fumble to reshape the contorted frames. Too upset to think right, I place the bent apparatus somewhere on my face.

Desperately, we all look for Cody. We don't see her lying dead in the street. This is a good thing, but where did she go?

A thunderous howl is heard, "Your horse took off down the driveway of that house!" The observer points to Stan and Connie's bungalow.

Chasing the trail, I sprint to the house. I can't believe this is happening! Adrenaline feeds my muscles strength beyond belief. My dusty denim sleeve mops up the leaky faucet trickling down. Fearfully I scan the street, worried about Cody's condition and whereabouts.

The weathered barn is a welcomed sight. I race pass the house and down the lengthy drive. Calmly, Cody waits at the corral gate, her head hung over the fence in anticipation of staying home. She turns around, looks at me, as if to say,

"What took you so long?"

My heart and lungs heave a huge sigh of relief at the sight of this ornery mare that I love. Despite what could have become a horrific tragedy, Cody and I remain safe. **Protected!**

Waves of emotion flood eyes and soul. Uncontrolled waterworks flow. Sleeve and handkerchief are synonymous. I want to strangle Cody, but refrain. Instead, she becomes the recipient of the biggest heartfelt hug humanly possible, at least by this human being.

"You gave me such a scare!" We could have become another splattered mess on the highway.

INSTEAD,

We became a lesson in God's protection

LESSON WELL TAUGHT

LESSON WELL LEARNED

Despite how our circumstances appeared... Both Cody and I were protected from a devastating event! My marriage is spiraling downward, so submission is not a subject I care to hear about right now, but...

If I remain submitted to God

I will be protected

The word "submission" formerly made the hair on my neck bristle. Odd how perspectives change. No longer do I see submission as a means of control.

Understanding brings appreciation.

Submission simply defined, "a **willingness** to yield or comply." It's not nearly as difficult or demanding as once presumed.

Some causes are bigger than us.

Life isn't always about us,

even though we think it is.

Funny,

the objects used for instruction

don't come at our choosing,

they just come.

Friends

15

In my humble opinion, forty-four degrees is comfortably perfect. Colorado isn't humid; we are dry as a desert. You can run horses without them lathering up as they do during hot summer months. Surprisingly, all a rider needs this time of year is a light-weight jacket.

Chocolate leaves let loose of their lifeline in autumn. Don't you love it? A feast for the senses! It's a fiery show of faded gold and merlot grasses gently clapping in the breeze. Mother Nature puts on a grand production! Sweet earthy aromas, wrinkled scarred trunks and scarlet brush weave a ruddy tapestry of visual and sensory overload.

"Cody, just because you're scared to ride alone, does not mean opportunities will pass us by. I've been told you like the boys, a lot. And you're the lead mare. Cody, what you need, is a companion." Seems kind of strange, a horse that takes the lead, yet fearful of her own shadow.

Horses come in all kinds of varieties, colors, ages and

sizes, anything you want. This grand quest for a companion just might resemble a rummage sale. Just how much money do I want to spend?

In the world of equine, a budget of $1,200 is pennies. It is what it is. Beyond that, what do I want? Hmm... Then I recall what Les at the dude ranch told me... Male, yes, Cody's friend needs to be a gelding. I don't want to deal with an unruly stud. A big guy, say sixteen hands high, would be nice. A well-trained horse, that can easily carry a person of any size and I don't really care about the breed. I'm not experienced enough to know one from another. He should handle well, be healthy and older, too. A young, quick horse is out of the question. Cody wants a companion, she can dominate.

Color, well, Les told me, "Don't buy a horse based on his color." I personally like flashy, but that doesn't make the horse any better or faster, just prettier to look at. We all can appreciate pretty, but,

Looks can be deceiving.

Spouses, cars, horses

are all the same.

Don't snag one based on appearances.

A poor selection outlasts looks.

OK, any color is fine, except the color of boring. That's my list. The race is on; let's go shopping!

"Yee-haw!" One might think that sounds really corny and stupid, but it's a great expression and loads of fun to say! Certainly yee-haw is not a glamorous word filled with any dignity, that's for darn sure. Maybe that's what I like about it. "Yee-haw!" Embarrassing for some, I know, but great fun, for those who embrace a good snort of levity now and then!

Numerous calls are made. Now that I have experience

under my belt, I feel confident to venture out, unsupervised. On my first outing, I spot a beautiful mustang in the herd with rare coloring called Gruella, otherwise known as a "ghost horse." He is exquisite and extremely unusual, primarily black with flicks of silver woven intermittently throughout his coat. But...he is not for sale; besides, he's a stud.

"NEXT!"

It's hard to capture time with children as they become more independent. I'm not blind! When an opportunity arises, snag it! "Sunshine, come with me. Help me find Cody a companion."

She states her terms, "Only if Bobby comes along!" The tall, handsome high-schooler holds a fancy to Sunshine. He's charming on one hand, sadistic and controlling on the other. Of course, Mom is not privy to his dark violent side.

We only think we have an agenda.

It can be altered at any time

by anything or anyone.

Our thinking is so limited.

This trip starts out to be all about the horse quest. It becomes readily apparent this adventure is **not** about the hunt. What transpires in the car is the true reason for today's excursion.

Bobby gets mad over some trivial thing as we drive down the road. The car is filled with deafening silence. It's an excruciating hour drive with nowhere to escape. Wow! I need to take advantage of this rare opportunity for a little one-on-one chat with my daughter. Interestingly enough, she has recently been dishing out this same cold shoulder treatment towards her father.

Cutting through the icy stillness our eyes connect through the rearview mirror. Our discussion unfolds, "Sunshine, tell me, how does this silent treatment make you feel?"

"I don't like it," bloodshot eyes shift to outdoors.

I probe further. "Does it make you feel loved or rejected?" After all, where is she going to go?

A stream rolls down her rosy cheeks as she whispers softly, "Rejected."

"How do you think your father feels when you give him the same silent treatment?"

"Rejected."

After a short time of reflection passes, I continue our little chat, "Sunshine, now that you know how it feels to be ignored and not spoken to, you might want to take care of matters with Papa when we get home."

I can see the light bulb come on, as her head bobs yes in the mirror.

Some lessons are difficult.

We don't like being on the receiving

end of what we dish out.

Be cognizant of the way you treat others,

It'll come back to you

and you may not like what you get!

Timing is everything. We arrive at our destination just as we wrap up our painful conversation. Oddly enough, we are only able to view the gelding from the road because the seller wouldn't bring the horse in from the pasture for us to see. Oh well, this trip wasn't about horses anyway.

"NEXT!"

I meet one seller at his corral in the foothills, shocked by the little horse standing before me. He's not much bigger than a pony. "He's a little guy," I comment, but what I'm really thinking is, either this seller's measuring stick is broke, or his vision is impaired. This little guy is a far cry from sixteen hands high.

"Ride him," he says.

I mount the Shetland. My legs practically drag the ground. After a couple of circles, he favors his right leg. Poor little fella. Really now! Shame on that man! Didn't his mama teach him any better? Lying don't do nobody no good. I know that's not proper English, but you get my point! Crooked horse trader!

Buyer beware!

Horse traders aren't known for their honesty.

They don't reveal what you should know.

Knowledge is power.

Think about this principle beyond horses.

You don't know what you don't know.

"NEXT!"

One ol' cowboy brings his nineteen-year-old buckskin gelding to the indoor arena at Westernaires. He's a big guy; the horse, that is. A gentle giant, he's approximately sixteen hands high. More of that equinese, I know. Just know he's REALLY big! I run my fingers through his coarse black mane and tail that stand out against his muscular golden sleek body. A black stripe trickles down the middle of his tailbone. He has a pleasant demeanor and seems well-mannered.

"What's his name?" I inquire of the slim, tall, rugged quiet soul.

"Sunny... Take him for a ride, ma'am," handing me the reins.

I ride the gentle giant around the arena. Yes, his size intimidates me, but he has a smooth gait. I believe he's a nice match for Cody. Besides, he's not for me.

"Will you give me a guarantee? I'd like to have my vet check him and if he's not OK, can I get my money back?"

"Sure," the cowboy warmly obliges, tipping his well-used hat. "I'll return your money." (I think he's a real cowboy. Not no wannabe.)

For whatever reason, I respond with a stiff poker face, "Will you deliver Sunny to the barn tonight?"

The cowboy nods. "Yep, and I'll throw in his saddle and bridle as a bonus." Playing it cool is the sign of a good poker player. (As if I know anything about poker.)

Refrained I remain, "Sold."

So that night, the quiet cowboy trailers the gelding to the barn. While saying his goodbyes, I hear him tenderly whisper in Sunny's ear, "They're going to spoil you here. Life will be good." On that note, he pats Sunny goodbye.

Cody is delighted! A friend! With a name like Sunny to brighten your day, who can resist? Cody's very own special friend! She is so excited. They chase up and down the fence with their heads high and stiff. Cody snorts wildly at Sunny while at the same time being cautious. It's quite humorous. Separated by a wooden fence, for their own protection, to become acquainted without injury. (I learned my lesson from the ranch.)

We'll see what the morning brings. It's been a long day. It's o'dark thirty and time to drag my weary butt home.

"Good night."

I slept real fast! You'd thought it was Christmas morning! I can't wait to get back to the barn. Beyond ecstatic, as a child's anticipation to see what Santa left under the tree.

Not only does Cody get a companion, I get a riding partner! What a blast! YEE-HAW!

Life is always more enjoyable shared

with a friend.

The sun has barely risen over the barn. Look at those two affectionately nuzzle. Relaxed and connected snouts hang over the fence. What a glorious morning for romance. You can see the love connection. Sorry we missed the mating dance. It would appear they didn't sleep a wink. Let the freedom bell ring! I can barely unlatch the gate before Cody pushes me out of her way! What a sight to behold, fresh love embraced. Cody acts all squirrelly, twisting her body wildly about, dancing over new-found love.

Rock solid Sunny is the man in charge. He's got that something, whatever "IT" is, I'm not sure, but he sure has "IT".

"Look what I've got." He holds his head high as he spreads his lips into a funny grin. Teeth in need of dental floss display his finer attributes for his prospective partner.

Cordially she returns the teeth-bearing grin. Confidence arises. Cody is a totally different horse this morning. *"I've got this handled, everything's OK. You can leave now. We want to be left alone,"* her attitude proudly conveys. *"I'm busy with more important interests right now; can't you see I'm entertaining a friend? He admires my teeth,"* she smiles real big.

With body language all my own, I walk away, mumbling under my breath, "Thanks would be nice."

Girls,

We do the same thing to our friends.

A male comes on the scene

and we push our friends to the curb.

Girlfriend,

Don't tell me you don't do the same thing.

It's time to find someone to ride with. To say I am thrilled would be an understatement!

"Sunshine, you want to be Mom's riding partner?" Hoping for a hearty "**yes!**"

"Maybe, but don't count on me, Mom." Hmm, I'm very disappointed, but not really surprised.

Her dad commonly uses the excuse of a bad back, "Don't count on me!" Not sure why I bothered to ask as we rarely do anything together anymore.

This is going to be harder than I thought. I don't have a normal work schedule; I'm off on Sunday, Monday and Tuesday and twist hair at the salon when most working people are off. What a brain tease. Someone in my circle must be available to ride.

Pondering friend options…

Deb comes to mind. She works nights and has days off. Deb is single, with no family attachments.

"Hey, Deb, do you want to ride?"

"Sure, anytime, I'd love to! Thanks."

With great enthusiasm, I question, "Do Mondays work for you?"

"You bet."

"YEE-HAW!" I now have a bona fide riding partner!

Am I ever psyched!

Sunny and Cody

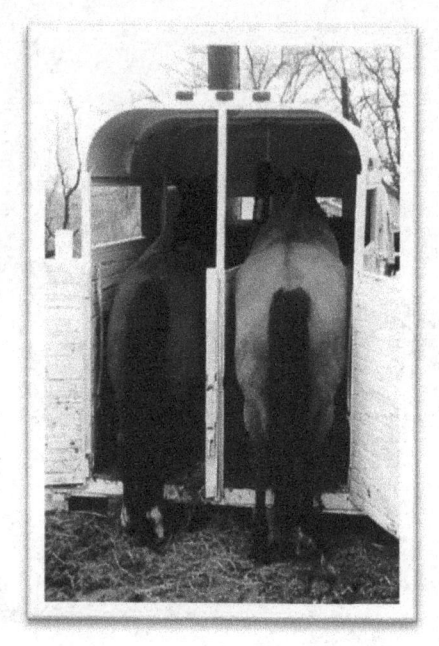

RB

Trailering

16

Life is wild on horseback. This city girl is chompin' at the bit. I'm ready to spread my wings and fly!

Instead, we are grounded. We have no trailer. It's time to change that or I'll bust! I don't have much money. Prices begin at $1,200 for an old, dilapidated one. After a long hunt, I find a butt-ugly horse trailer in the ski town of Frisco. It isn't pretty. In fact, it's a sorry ol' thing, but it's only 350 bucks! Brakes are frozen. It needs paint and some tires, and a brand spankin' new floor. Aw, what's a little time and labor? Ben can do all the improvements. And he did. A few weeks later the trailer dazzles like new!

"Yee-haw!" I burst with pure joy!

Excited, we drive to the barn. Load those ponies up and ride somewhere, anywhere we haven't been before, which leaves it wide open. Ben, Sunshine and I are so proud of our sparkling snow-white trailer.

We're off on our first outing. This is merely for pleasure and to grasp understanding of trailering. The horses brace themselves as I steer around the corner.

At the sound of hooves stumbling about on the new wood-planked floor, Sunshine yells, **"M – O – M ! ! ! S – L – O – W   D – O –W – N !"** We feel horses shift weight, clunking from one side to the other.

Ben astutely recommends, "Your driving habits need to be altered, at least when you're hauling horses."

"A little less heavy on the foot, is a good idea too, Mom," Sunshine adds.

With each outing we stretch our distance just a little further. There is a lot to learn about trailering horses. You'd think one could just jump in and go. It's not that simple. Some people are oblivious to the complexities involved in trailer maneuvers.

Trailers are a beast to park,

get out of tight spots, or awkward predicaments.

Trailers take practice.

Lots of practice. Some never get it.

Hooves stumble when going around corners too fast. Your camper or motor home might not complain, but horses don't care for it much. It takes a lot of experience, especially in backing up a trailer. Have you heard of jack-knifed? It's easy to do.

White Ranch is an exceptional spot to ride. It's close to Golden Gate Park. Today's excursion is Deb's and my first. Oh my! The views that lie before us! You can reach out and touch Denver's skyline. How spectacular! You think you're in the high country but you're not. Trails are everywhere, some steep and rocky, others gentle, rolling hills lined with tall, beautiful grass. Check out this stream with a corral nearby. How exciting is this! I gasp in awe with visions of overnight campouts on horseback. White Ranch is our new favorite park to explore.

Horses sense rustling in the grass on this warm autumn afternoon. Like soldiers on high alert, abruptly, Sunny and Cody stop in their tracks! Heads rise, ears rotate as radars before coming to a standstill. We listen and wait for that which has caught their attention to reveal itself.

"OOOPS! Sorry." Under our very noses, surprised as much as the young lovers clothed only by tall grass.

When you're caught with your pants down

you should stay down!

"Oh, that's nothing to be concerned about," we reassure the horses, and trot off snickering.

Wildlife comes in various forms!

Keep those peepers wide open.

The sun gently drops behind the mountains. This day needs a grand finale! A treat of sorts is placed on the food bin shelf in the trailer's front. Tired horses are unsaddled. I lead Cody to the gate, and guess what? You guessed it, what a surprise, she refuses to walk in. Grand finale gone awry!

JUST GREAT! We stand there bewildered, contemplating what to do.

"Sunny, get in the trailer!" He steps right up. "You are such a good horse, Sunny," rewarding him with a gentle pat to his enormous, toned rump.

"Let's try again, Cody, come on. It's your turn."

"NO, YOU CAN'T MAKE ME! I DON'T WANNA GO HOME!" She's one determined horse! What does one do with such an attitude?

Cody refuses every attempt to load. The temperature has dropped, it's getting late and the park will close soon. We must leave.

"I'm not spending the night; you might want to stay Cody, but I don't!" I reprimand my naughty mare, but to no avail. She could care less.

Earlier, we passed a small corral at the top. There is no alternative but to leave Cody and Sunny in the pen, with no padlock. This makes me real nervous. Anyone could steal, release or torment them!

"I'll return tomorrow with a trainer to get you guys home; that is, if you're still here! Hope you don't starve."

Apprehensively we jump into the truck and drive the empty trailer out of the park. There is no other choice. Cody got her way. I don't like it, not one bit! I'm sure she's proud of herself.

Down the mountain we proceed. In front of the truck darts, not just one, but **two** mountain lions. I'm telling you, real live **cougars!** The four-legged hunter type!

"Good Lord, did you see that?" I've lived in Colorado all my life and I have never seen mountain lions before today!

"Oh yeah! I see them. WOW!" Deb is as dumb struck as I am. "They're magnificent!"

We stop in the middle of the road to admire the rare sight. The male is HUGE, sleek and lightly speckled. He spans at least ten feet in length. Following close behind is a smaller beautiful black female, not small mind you, just smaller. The pair shoots straight up this incredibly steep embankment, in the direction we just left. Yikes! As if I wasn't worried enough! Now with good reason, I have a deeper sense of trepidation!

Do mountain lions eat horses? Do they attack for sport? The possibilities scare me. I just witnessed how incredibly agile and light-footed those animals are.

My anxiety level is elevated; my palms stick to the steering wheel. Every nerve in my body tenses up. Horses are big animals. Will my two defend themselves? Could horses kill their predator? I don't know.

"Lord, please keep them safe. Protect them."

It'll be late morning before our trainer can meet us.

It's a long sleepless night. I'm fearful and worried, toss and turn the night away. So much so, that my teeth clench. I expect my jaw to lock up by morning. Will I find horses safe, injured or missing?

A knowledgeable, gifted trainer has been hired. Yeah, I know, it took me long enough. Pam is a young, gentle soul referred to me by someone to whom I'm forever indebted. If I could only remember who that was... hum. Well, eleven o'clock is our meeting time.

Anxiously, I travel back to the mountain. To my relief, both are alive and hungry. Thank God they weren't someone's midnight snack!

Release what you pray, you'll sleep better

or worry all night, because

you don't totally trust God for the outcome.

It's a personal choice.

It's discouraging to take Cody anywhere. Cooperation to load is always there, but when it's time to go home, she balks. Does she hate her home? What's up with the obstinate behavior? Truly, we need a trainer!

Pam rescues us. Her small frame matches her gentle nature. Kind, caring and a soft whip are her methods. In a matter of minutes, Pam concludes, "There is nothing wrong with Cody and her trailer ability. IT'S YOU!"

Ouch. "Me, huh?" I knew that. Sherrie never spoke of a trailer problem.

Pam gives me a verbal spanking. "Yep, it's you. **You are the one in need of training**. Cody goes in the trailer just fine!"

"Well, OK then, teach me."

We meet over the course of several weeks at the nearby arena. Pam has a big job to undo bad behavior, which Cody has gotten away with for some time. Hope she's successful.

It's like rearing kids,

it's not until it's too late

that you realize you messed them up for life!

After all, kids don't pop out of the womb

with a training manual.

"Cody needs to know who's boss. She's done a great job

of training you. Cody has you buffaloed into thinking she won't get into the trailer. Here's what we're going to do..." Pam takes command and stands in the middle of the arena with whip in hand. Cody responds immediately to the whip's crack and trots around the edge of the corral. Trainers double click combined with a snapped whip results in a faster gait. When Pam wants Cody to slow down, she simply steps forward. What an amazing process to watch! This is all very familiar. Sherrie and Cody rehearsed this identical routine.

Pecking order is a natural process

in the animal kingdom.

For that matter,

amongst humans as well.

Pam completes the exercise, slowly approaches Cody, and gently rubs the bridge of her nose. At the same time, Pam rewards her with a treat and words of encouragement, then turns and slowly walks away. Cody follows. Beat me with a wooden stick!

AMAZING...

How a little respect in a gentle manner,

benefits a relationship of any type,

spouse, parent, child, employee or boss.

"Reneé, now you do it." Pam orders, "If Cody doesn't do what you want, then run her in a small circle and try it again."

Explicitly, I follow her directions. Every week we expand upon the previous lesson, helping me to gain Cody's respect. It takes a while to reestablish seniority. Within a few months and several excursions under our belt, Cody's level of cooperation is much improved.

Amongst the herd

respect comes after authority is established!

Battles are the process for creating top dog positions.

Not to be redundant,

you know the routine by now.

Humans and horses are a lot alike.

Caution thrown to the wind. Eagerness and readiness reign supreme. Dreams await this cowgirl wannabe seeking adventure! The scenic Yampa Valley offers it all! Weekend warriors can indulge in any of these delicious options, from rodeos, river rafting, naked hot spring to world-class skiing and of course, trail-blazing! Duh! Almost peed myself just thinkin' about it! Steamboat, or bust!

Right smack in the center of town you'll spot the rodeo grounds. Don't let the ball caps and tennis shoes fool you. Under those ordinary workin' man clothes are real cowboys! They hang out at the rodeo grounds to discuss bulls, ladies, beer and chew. Would you look at this! Authentic rodeo accommodations for my favorite riding compadres. Yes, of course we verified it was okay. I'm feelin' lightheaded! A super-hip cow town surrounded with real rodeo dudes! Awe...let the sweet urban cowgirl savor the moment!

Sunny and I stretch our weary traveled legs in the arena. His body responds with such pleasure, as if the surroundings are familiar to him. Not that I know anything, it's those subtle cues, that tell his heartwarming story. As soon as we enter the rodeo arena, his gait and head perk up. Sunny checks out the bleachers and the pen with confidence. He's right at home, looking around, recalling an exciting time in his past. I'd bet my bottom dollar, Sunny has been here before!

Winter Olympic athletes train above the rodeo grounds, on Howelsen Hill. It's the ski spot used mostly by locals. Shhhhh... don't tell anyone, it's a secret that won't siphon the checkbook! Come summer, these rugged slopes transform into horseback trails. The hillside serves as tonight's vantage point to gaze upon cute cowboys who chase big bulls! Stick around, watch festive fireworks explode in the star lit sky. This is cow-town at its best!

You just missed it! That bull charged the clown! Hope he's okay. Bulls are like that; destruction paves their path. Taken' what's not theirs for the taken'. I saw it all! Could have been worse than a busted gored arm. Don't know the draw, clown blood or his colorful outfit? I guess it's all part of a day's work as a rodeo clown, cheating death.

Can you tell, Steamboat is my favorite spot in Colorado? What a dream! I'm beside myself. Happy dance eruption!

One last stop before heading home, our beloved Rabbit Ears Pass. Embrace the moment, just look at the majestic, rugged mountains as far as your eye can see. Views from the top of the world are magnificent! The clear cloudless sky is marine blue. A hint of pine floats on the crisp breeze. Do you smell it? See the wildflowers jump with elation? Soak up God's Sanctuary. This trip is just as much spiritual as it is natural.

What an honor and privilege to ride

and admire His creation.

Trampling through knee-high-grass on horseback, we speculate the massive rabbit ears are within our grasp. Yet those ears elude Ben and me, bummer. It's further than we thought. Daylight's a burnin'. It's back to the grindstone tomorrow. We turn around and head to the trailer.

With horses unsaddled, we gather our gear and greet weekend stragglers. Not too many people remain. What a glorious peaceful getaway. What more can we ask?

How about horses that load?

She did it again! I can't believe it! Fire burns! Steam spews! Flame's torch loose flying words from these hot lips!

"Cody, I wouldn't have brought you all this distance if I thought you wouldn't load! What is wrong with you, girl?"

We go round and round in circles behind the trailer reestablishing who's boss. Ben, Sunshine and I each take turns trying to load Cody. A fresh face with a different demeanor and approach surely will benefit the cause.

A couple of giggling kids are intrigued, as they watch our meager attempt to load an insubordinate mare. Our efforts are futile. A pathetic moment of sheer embarrassment.

People don't like to be told what to do.

Horses don't either,

even if it's a great idea.

They want it to be their own.

You know, like men.

Right, men?

Three hours later she casually walks into the trailer on her own accord. I want to smack her! But it's getting late. We have a long way to go.

"BRAT!"

A Spirited Mare

Who can reign?

Is the object of this spirited being
to control or enjoy?

Must she be a challenge to conquer?
Or a tool from which I learn?

May my eyes be open
to the lessons brought forth
by this beautiful spirited mare of mine.

ST

Hall Ranch

17

Winter in Colorado is often mild and dry. The natives keep it a secret for population control. To our dismay, the word has leaked out. We are not always buried in six feet of snow and long cold spells as rumored. It's common in the dead of winter to find hardy natives parading around in shorts. Today, is an extraordinary sunny and warm winter's day. A great day to unleash our wild side!

Enthusiasm transcends phone lines. "I've researched

options for someplace different to ride. We should try Hall Ranch, near Lyons." Deb outshines my venturesome side, hands down.

"Where's Lyons?"

"It's just on the north side of Boulder. It'll be fun. We have all day, right?"

I wonder if it really matters as to where the ranch is. "Sure, let's do it. Meet you at the barn in a half hour."

Hurriedly, I lace up my Ariats, snatch my Australian duster and grab my bent-up ol' outback hat by the crown. Keys in hand I cinch the crumpled hat's dry leather neck strings as I bolt through the door.

My friend is gifted with gentle pressure to push me beyond my comfort zone. She gets us off the beaten path. If left to my own devices, I'd probably dig a rut in the path, never straying far. How boring is that? I know. I can't believe it myself. Why would anyone be content with normal or boring? Cody is anything but!

If you give a horse freedom

it will return to the barn,

or the original starting place.

With unprecedented speed, Deb and I load horses and tack. We always travel light. A water bottle, a jacket, a wad of tissue and a snack is all we need. Oh, and don't forget the Leatherman tool for emergencies. The small saddle horn bag holds most of our gear. Shed jackets are rolled-up then bound with leather straps behind each saddle. You can forget cell phones. Rarely is there any service in the backcountry.

We only have a few hours to ride. The sun sets by four-thirty. Basking in the glory of the brisk winter escapade, we saddle woolly horses ready to explore. A sign posted at the trailhead entrance catches our attention.

"WARNING: MOUNTAIN LION SPOTTED IN THIS AREA!"

Horses are equipped with extraordinary abilities to see and hear beyond what is humanly possible. This is truly reassuring when you're alone in the backcountry.

We climb in elevation and stumble upon a large herd of deer. Their solitude is disrupted by intruding city slickers. One would think that when humanoids sneak upon wild game, the deer would jump up and disappear. Some do, but the manner they flee is the darndest thing I've ever seen. Animation in motion. Some flatten like a pancake and dart between the wires, others leap straight-legged upward over the fence. Many remain calm, unthreatened by our presence. We wait, engage in a stare-down. Nervous black marble eyes glare. Is this a challenge of courage or to see who will fold first? We grow weary of the silly game and move on.

Venturing off the beaten path, we discover a charming old stone house that looks like it was built in the late eighteen hundreds. Smooth river rocks could certainly stand to be "freshened up" with new mortar. The old chimney barely hangs on. Oh, what history must hide behind those old walls?

"What a great place for a picnic lunch when we have more time."

"Another day, maybe." Deb replies as horse and rider saunter off.

After a while, the rolling hills melt into each another. What direction are we going? Cloud overcast has crept overhead, so we can't determine which way is west. We set off in one direction, thinking it's the way to the parking lot. Ok, turn around and try the opposite direction.

A compass and a book displaying

edible wild berries could prove to be invaluable.

Those two items should be added to our supply list. Let's call them S4S or supplies for survival. S4S are nowhere to be found in them there hills. Time to get creative and drop the reins. "Whew!" We don't need no stinkin' compass or berry book, we have horses! Cody and Sunny turn around and take us in the right direction, hopefully.

Allowing horse sense to take over

is a great alternative to poor planning.

Overcome with brilliance, thinkin' we are all that... we let the horses settle into a noticeably faster pace. Shortly after, we stumble upon a fellow traveler quickly descending on his mountain bike. He confirms our course of action is correct. Sure enough, the horses are spot-on with their keen sense. As if we had any doubt.

Horses have an innate sense of direction

unlike their human counterparts,

I tend to believe a horse cannot get lost.

Time eludes us. Temperature drops. It's nearly four o'clock and no parking lot in sight.

Abruptly, the horses stop. Antennas at full alert! Ears zero in on the subject at large. Necks stiffen, and heads rise. We listen and wait.

"What do you see, Cody?" I whisper.

Up over the ridge walking toward us is a diminutive older gal sporting lightweight shorts, and a depleted water bottle. She has no jacket or sweater, nothing on her but a small fanny pack and a panicked face.

"Can you tell me the direction to the parking lot?" the hiker quivers.

"Oh, lady, you are a long way from the lot, plus you're going the wrong direction," Deb divulges.

Tears well up in the soft blues of the bewildered, woman. "I've been walking for some time. A hiker told me this was the correct direction to the lot," pointing forward she chokes back emotions. "I have no water and I'm trying to get back to my car."

Deb graciously offers her a lift. Without hesitation the offer is accepted. They grab hands and Deb pulls the little gal up on Sunny's backside.

En route to the trailhead, we discuss the unlikelihood of our paths crossing. The lost lady embraces relief from being afoot. "I kept asking God for help," the woman recalls her story of desperation. "The trail was deserted. I was scared and cold."

You'd've thought the flood gates opened as tears flow. We're all a mess.

When in higher altitude

even if it's nice when you start out,

you need a jacket and plenty of water.

Don't be deceived by the warmth of the day.

Temperatures can drop quickly.

Times like now, for instance.

What could have been a tragic incident instead resulted in two paths intertwining to rescue a chilly lost soul. The combination of dropped temperatures, mountain lions and a lack of preparation was a recipe for disaster. All three of us couldn't help but reflect, what are the odds of this glorious outcome?

Just before dusk, we deliver one grateful lady to her car with a story of divine intervention deposited deep into her soul.

To be a godsend for someone in need,

what a privilege!

It'll come when you least anticipate it!

Crossing the Platte

18

Catch a glimpse of relaxed horses sunning. Spoiled is easy to envy. Look at them, not a care in the world, curled up in a ball, soaking up the warmth. Basking melts away all of life's anxieties, that is, should a horse have any.

We should take note,

slow down, relax and give

sun therapy a try.

It might make us easier to be around.

I've intruded.

"Oh...it's you...This can only mean one thing, work."

I prefer to call it play. After all, fun is why I'm here. They know this. Nonchalantly the two lift their heads in unison from their earthen bed. *"If we must, we'll go with you."*

"Come on, guys." I emphasize with a loud clap, "I hate to disturb your peace; break time is over. Get up! Let's go!"

Slowly they roll back and forth like dough kneaded on a marble slab to massage sore warm backs. Gradually both tilt to their sides and extend their long flailing legs. In unison, the two progress to their knees, before rising from a serious nap. With a brisk shake they ascend, covered in a dusty billow. The scene resembles an awe-striking, glorious movie. You know, where the light shines through the dense fog from behind the powerful team of majestic horses. Resurrection has occurred!

~~~~

Anytime we introduce horses to a new environment, heads go up with excitement, and anticipation. Horse sense kicks into overdrive until they relax.

Stop, listen and sniff.

Danger is recognized

through a keen sense of awareness.

Wildlife comes in many forms, bicycles, people, animals and unfamiliar noises. When comfort comes, horses' heads and tails lower to a natural relaxed position, where the neck horizontally levels out with the body.

We have an entire day to ride alongside the canyon trails. The earth explodes with great visual effects, from belly-high brush to knee-high-grass. Wonderful sounds and aromas harmonize like a beautiful symphony. Wood scents delicately blend with fragrant wildflowers. Chorus birds chirp. Crickets faintly rub their stringed instruments. Flies and bees add to the concerto, an insistent buzz. The Platte River embellishes the orchestra landscape! Colorado at its best! Let the music of summer begin.

Expectations run high as we've been told just how lovely the canyon is. Majestic veils of color are envisioned to drape steep walls of a lovely narrow canyon with a woodsy path following a creek. Instead it's a wide dirt road, riddled with pedestrian traffic! "Bummer, how disappointing is this?" Not at all what we had signed up for on a lazy Monday? What's up with that? The advantage of not riding on the weekend is, trails are fairly private. But today you'd think there was a party in the canyon.

Not that I don't like people; because I do. My experience has taught me, however, that people and horses don't share the path well. Urbanites just aren't very horse savvy. They are unaware of the dos and don'ts of horse etiquette, me included. That is, up until now. Horse etiquette is not taught outside of the equine community. Why is that? We teach about other animal behaviors. Children are instructed not to pet other people's animals until permitted. You never know who is friend or foe. You can't assume every four-legged critter is accepting of humanoids.

Pranksters think it's amusing to spook a horse.

Even if accidental,

it can be extremely dangerous

putting those nearby at risk, including the spook-er.

Horses don't take kindly to noisy kids on bikes. An undesirable outcome could be had. Mine are vulnerable to startling or, should I say, Cody is. For everyone's safety, Deb redirects the reins. "Let's check out the trails down by the river." Without hesitation Sunny turns around and blazes the way to the riverbed.

Not a soul in sight. Peaceful, harmonious solitude supplies all the proper elements for a majestic summer serenade. What song would *you* sing if no one was listening? It's OK to fearlessly belt out your favorite song, you know you want to. We're not shy. We let her loose, delivering a soulful chorus. Harmonizing hums replace escaping words. I know this all sounds rather corny, but the surroundings call for it. We disrupt the tranquil banks with our groove in motion as we charge the horses, gleefully belting our songs through the brush. The trail is narrow, only wide enough for a single horse. If Sunny slows down, Cody is right on top of him, her head rests directly on his hindquarters. His ears lie down flat against his head. He doesn't take to it kindly. Their spat disrupts our musicality.

"Back off, Cody."

Oh, what great fun! Spontaneous laughter adds a harmonic element woven into the canyon's symphony.

No doubt, Deb and Sunny have become impressively connected. Sunny is everything I could have hoped for. He's big, agreeable, laid-back, well-mannered and well-trained. He's extraordinary.

Sunny gives Cody the lead when she wants it; if not, she'll take it from him! *"Move over, I've got it handled!"* is Cody's approach, as she crowds her way to the front, although on this trip, there is no competition. Sunny is "top dog" all the way.

"Let's cross the river," Deb suggests.

"You do know Cody's afraid of water, right?"

"Well, let's work with her."

We spot what seems to be a reasonable edge to gracefully transition into the river, or so we think. Sunny lunges in! Closely we follow with a gentle kick to Cody's belly. She takes a small step. Cody wants to please. Chilly encapsulates wet hooves. Reverse erupts. It's Showtime! The musical hip-hop dance routine belts out the familiar song, *"I'm not goin' down the darn river!"* She whinnies, *"you can't make me! Not now, not ever! No-no-no-o-o, I ain't goin'!"* Bellows her soulful rhythmic argument.

My oh my, I'm hardly surprised, "Deb, come back!" I yell. "We need a closer lead."

The blessed cavalry returns to take full charge. There is nothing gradual about the drop at the water's edge. Without batting an eye, Sunny lunges down the embankment to assure our rescue.

"Look, Cody, it's easy, no worries. Watch me! This is how you do it."

This bold mare is intimidated by the river yet refuses to be left behind. Hopefully she won't freak out over belly deep water. We follow right on Sunny's haunches as if he carries us across on his back. Unexpectedly, Cody remains calm, as if it's no big deal. It's not that she can't do it; she just needs a big strong male to hold her hand, so to speak. Let's face it; she's a chicken at heart!

Humans sometimes are like that.

We need someone who walks in authority

to take the lead and direct us.

Let's face it, we, too, are chicken.

Long legs disappear into the deep. Like flies on manure, gnats swarm. What a challenge to keep this mouth shut, as lips flap as fast as water flows. The river creeps up to the horses' bellies! Yikes! Boots and stirrups pop up to withhold thirsty leather! Horses do swim, don't they? Don't tell me they don't!

This unsettling experience takes me back to the source of my own reluctance of fast moving water. It was supposed to be a lazy family float trip down the Yampa River. My sister Denise, her husband Kevin and their two little girls joined our family. We gathered at the river entry just before the bend. Waiting our turn, we eavesdropped on the rafting guide firing off crucial survival tips. A listen-up moment. "Stay to the right of the river's fork. The rapid is too dangerous on the left. In the event we capsize,

"Go down the river feet first.

if you become sucked under the water,

push off with your feet!"

The family reiterated plans to meet at the hot spot on the right side of the river's bend before shoving off the bank's edge. Six-year-old special-needs Jessica departed with her daddy at the helm. Close behind, Denise manhandles their yellow lab puppy on a leash and four-year-old daughter, Katrina. In a loaded two-man rubber raft, they slipped into the river. Sis's family all had lifejackets, we did not. Sunshine and I followed close behind with our bottoms nestled in fancy store bought inner tubes. You know the type? With handles on the sides. Ben's fear of water kept him on shore, nursing his cold coffee.

We watched Kevin and Jessica safely arrive at the destination point as the strong current pushed my daughter and I closer to the wrong side of the river. In horror we watched Denise's raft capsize over violent eddies at the fork! Cadence was swallowed up by the vortex! The boat's rope was tightly looped around Katrina's little neck. My niece's terrified baby blues bulged helplessly through the brush! That was the last we saw before the current swiftly carried the remaining mortified participants into the "forbidden" zone. Yes, the one we were indirectly told to avoid.

The rapids increased in strength. I felt helpless to bring the nightmare to an end. In a panic, I began to pray.

Moving water cannot be reasoned with.

You're just along for the ride.

Ahead was my chance to pull away from the current. The water appeared shallow under the upcoming bridge. Instead, the inner tube refused to let me go! What a fight! A huge column separated Sunshine and me. Her tube popped out the other side, but no Sunshine. Not knowing where she was, I screamed her name! Time stood still. Screams met silence. Hours seemed to pass before Sunshine walked on water into her father's arms. How Ben happened to be there at the right time to embrace Sunshine, I'll never know. I was relieved to know she made it out alive before the current ripped me away.

Cold, sore hands tightly clasped stripped willow leaves hanging over the banks edge in the attempt to pull myself ashore. Worn to a frazzle, how we narrowly escaped the brutal adventure, is beyond me. It's a miracle any of us survived.

Enjoy river rafting

with the assistance of professionals.

~~~~~

I have no lifejacket on today; for crying out loud, I'm horseback riding! One action-packed river experience is more than enough to fill my repertoire, thank you very much!

I have huge empathy for Cody as we both hesitate to cross the scary river. Sweat drips from my brow. We trudge downstream like old pros. Cody settles into the river walk.

A milestone accomplished! Hands smack together high in the air in celebratory fashion upon our safe arrival to the center island. WOW! What a relief. What a surprise! Slap me silly!

Surprises come when you least expect them!

Maybe that is why

they're called a surprise.

Horses ferociously shake off! Now that's a wild spin!

When life sends you through the spin cycle

stand up,

hold your head high and do it again!

Hang on tight!!

Deb exhibits nerves of steel and more horse sense than me. She sure is good on the backside of a horse. They make a great team, not at all in need of therapy, unlike Cody and yours truly.

We wander in circles on the tiny island, dodging branches around the haunted forest smack dab in the middle of the river. There is no trail. I shudder at the creepy sense of danger. I'm not sure what Deb and Sunny think, but I'm thinking we should turn around. It's eerie! There could be creatures lurking, ready to suck unsuspecting humanoids down-under, never to be seen again. That kind of creepy!

"Let's get out of here!" Quivering lips and shifty eyes unveil my soul's uneasiness. The only escape is through the river.

Deb and Sunny take the lead. There's no discussion before they quietly disappear into the murky water.

"How can they do this to us again?" Not wanting to be left behind, Cody picks up the pace right up to the bank's edge, when she breaks out her dance and gut-wrenching chorus line, *"AIN'T NO WAY I'M GETTIN' WET! AIN'T NO WAY I'M GOIN' DOWN! YOU CAN'T MAKE ME, NO, NO, NO, NO MATTER HOW HARD YOU TRY... NO MATTER HOW HARD YOU TRY!"*

Can you feel her soulful cry?

So can I!

Not to be outdone, Goofy receives a determined squeeze. Between shallow breaths, seeking a divine intervention of any type, self-therapy is administered. "Relax. Don't panic, it could be worse; you could be tubing down the Yampa. There is no reason for distress. Stop it, Reneé! Just breathe!" When this is all over, they will either tranquilize me with a shot or two of whiskey or institutionalize me. That is, if I survive!

"You aren't getting away with that nonsense again, Cody." Feverishly I beat on her belly as if she were a drum! I should've seen it coming. Reluctance repeats the same chorus line.

"AIN'T NO WAY." She backs up again. Cody stands her ground, *"DON'T LEAVE ME!"* her soulful melody sings outs.

There is a healthy fear

that keeps us safe from danger.

Then there is a fear that keeps us

from enjoying life.

Determine the difference.

Don't allow fear to imprison you!

By now, Deb and Sunny are on the other side of the river. Calmly, they saunter past the phantom creatures of the deep, promenading their way through the brush. They never look back to see if we made it safely across or got sucked into the black hole. No, they proceed as if all is well with the world.

"Hey! Friend!" bellows Cody with a stiff shake from beneath the saddle, *"DON'T LEAVE US! Wait!"*

Loudly I shout out the alleged interpretation, "Come back! Cody refuses to cross!"

Possibly perturbed, Deb and Sunny cross back again to rescue us once more. She never voices her thoughts, but I can imagine what they are. I bet you can too.

Cody's body language implies she has had enough for one day. *"Let's just stay here, OK?"*

"Get a grip! We are not spending the night! We've got to get off this island! Let's just do it!" I stroke Cody's lathered, arched neck to instill encouragement and confidence. The ol' pat on the back, you can do it, comforting mom trick.

When in doubt or scared

do it anyway!

Close your eyes if you have to.

Just do it scared!

Apprehensively, Cody and I wait for our escort. This is no easy task, to muster up the courage to reenter the mysterious black hole. We are in repeat mode, reciting the same chorus line, annoyed by the skipping record. Travel in circles, we're stuck in repeat. Why we don't fall over dizzy, I'll never know. Thank God, our redeemer has come!

"Deb, let Cody get right on Sunny's haunches before you enter the water."

Deb acknowledges with a smile and a nod.

Everyone needs a redeemer

at some point in their lives.

We just need to ask.

Splash! With our first step, we drop steeply off the ledge. So much for a gentle incline. Once again, the water is up to the horses' bellies. I'm not certain what to expect. I can only hope to survive.

Sunny is a steady ol' plow, trudging through the sandy riverbed. Impressive he is. *"I do this all the time, no worries, mate."* Sunny, synonymous for nerves of steel.

Cody, on the other hand, performs a bluesy river dance. What she lacks in rhythm and grace, she more than makes up with plenty of soul! We could soon fall off the pages of this beautiful sheet music and be forced to swim for our lives!

Nothing would surprise me more, except what happened. Uneventfully we cross the river. I know. Can you believe it? Cody's dramatic river dance minus the exciting crescendo! It takes the wind right out of your sails, doesn't it? It does mine. On one level, it seems to be a rather dull conclusion to an otherwise extraordinary Monday morning. Slap me silly! A surprise party on me! Jubilant relief erupts. "Oh Cody, you are so funny!"

You just never know who will rise

to the occasion when you least imagine it!

You know...

like kids and spouses

when given a chance,

they'll often surprise you.

Rattled nerves recover after an infusion of belly laughter. Cody and I have passed the river test by the skin of our teeth. The morning ride continues with pleasure of the quiet ordinary sort. We cross the river several more times on this hot summer day. Cody is an old pro after the first few episodes. All is forgotten. We move forward.

Conquer your fear!

By doing so,

you may learn to enjoy the thing

you feared the most.

Our intended rendezvous point on the Yampa

TV

The Park

19

The salon door swings wide open. Overwhelmed by pungent aromas and a swarm of elderly ladies, Mike contemplates his safety. Strands of thick curly blond hair could be mobbed by jealous old ladies. Anything is possible to a well-dressed man who dares to enter the salon on a busy Friday morning. Endangerment never deters Mike from selling ads at this fine salon.

Jay Leno poked fun at one of Mike's ads during a segment on the Tonight Show. Thanks to Jay, my friend's magazine became an overnight sensation!

"Mike, let's convene in the backroom." I know he's here

to sell advertising, but I have other plans. "Hey Mike, come horseback riding with me." It doesn't take much to persuade. Typically, the response is a hearty yes, but it never happens. This time is different. I wrestle Mike down for a date.

Busy lives get in the way of living,

if you let them.

"How about in two weeks? Monday the seventeenth? Nine a.m. at The Park, does that work for you?"

With a twinkle of enthusiasm, Mike bobs his sandy long curls in acceptance of my exciting invitation.

Early on the seventeenth, I rise. There's lots of ground to cover before nine o'clock. The horses eat while I load tack, hay and the glorious bribery tool, the beloved grain.

Daylight's a-burnin'! Adventures scream, "come hither!" Excited to ride "The Park," I stop to pay at the entry gate. The young attendant inside the cramped booth hands me a map. Enthusiastically I tell him, "This is my first time here!" Words fall on deaf ears. Too early in the morning for small talk, I guess.

A simple slap leaves my lips as I drive away, "Well, OK, then." Whatever happened to pleasant congeniality?

Having received no help from the gatekeeper, I pull over to the side and wait for Mike. I am a woman left to her own devices! Scanning "The Park's" map, I see no horse trail markings or trailer parking.

This popular destination, appreciated for its diverse amenities, includes riding stables. The Park was built for damage control after the flood years ago, thus I will now refer to it as The Dam Park. People replenish their souls on a blistering hot summer day with boats, jet skis, horses, bicycles and camping. Weekend action melts away into a serene ordinary Monday.

Mike is right on time. He follows me to a shady paved spot on the west side, where we unload horses. Mike is not a horseman, nor is he familiar with the saddle routine, so while I saddle both horses, I fire off riding instructions.

"Mike, keep your heels down, half of your weight in the saddle, the other half in your feet. This will help with balance. Not too tight on the reins, keep them loose. It'll hurt Sunny's mouth, he doesn't like that much. Hold the reins close to the saddle horn, not at your chest or in the air. Don't slap your butt around in the saddle. Instead, get the feel of Sunny's rhythm. Think of him as your dancing partner; it'll serve you both much better."

"Got it? Any questions? Ready?"

Mike's head bobs and eyes glaze over. He has no concept of what I just told him. He is probably wondering, "What language is this?"

Yeah, right! How could I expect anyone to grasp a sixty-second explanation, the skills that took me years to acquire?

We mount up and begin our journey through the coolness of the trees along the path parallel the lake.

Hardly anyone is here today, so we pick up the pace and blaze the trail near the lake's edge. About a half hour into our run, a park ranger hunts us down in his camouflaged hunt mobile.

"HEY!" the ranger yells at us. **"You aren't allowed to have the horses anywhere near the water! You need to get out of here!"** He sternly orders us about as if we are under his military command.

Both of us are stunned by his demeaning approach. "Who does he think he is?"

"He sure was nasty, wasn't he?" Mike comments with his thick brow raised. "Maybe they should mark the trails."

"Do you think? They assume we are mind readers. I've never experienced such hostility. I'm not quite sure what to do with that."

Mike's cocked head emphasizes both of our sentiments.

"If such rules exist, they should post them along the path," I snarl at the injustice dealt out.

We spot a path in the grassy area away from the lake. On occasion, I peek over my shoulder to observe Mike's equinese assimilation. The lesson just didn't stick. He's bouncing around in the saddle with the reins held high in the air. It's quite amusing; maybe not to Sunny or Mike, but it is to me.

"Hey, Mike," I yell, "feel the rhythm; think of it as a dance. Move with your partner's cadence, not against him; you'll both be much happier. Your butt will appreciate it too."

I don't think Mike connected with anything I told him, but we can still have a great time kickin' up dust, lopin' through the park, even if he slaps against the saddle the whole time. Unfortunately, the horse is taking the brunt of it all. Sorry, Sunny.

Twenty minutes later, that's right, you guessed it! The terminator of fun hunts us down once again in his camo killer mobile, this time disguised as a dam hostile ranger.

"I told you not to ride anywhere near the lake!"

Evidently, we are not far enough away from the lake; just how far is far anyway? Maybe I'm blind in one eye and can't see out of the other, but I don't see the lake anywhere.

The interrogation continues. **"Is that your trailer parked on the west side?"**

"Yes," is my annoyed response, "what's wrong now?"

"You can't park there!" he throws his authority around like he's manhandling a bale of hay!

Is harassment his form of guilty pleasure? I've had it by now! Tired of being pushed around, I can feel my blood pressure ready to spike near the stroke level. It takes a lot to push me over the edge, as I'm generally even-tempered. This power-hungry man obviously has nothing better to do than harass a couple of riders. I find no pleasure in his lording authority to bully taxpayers with a Park badge, as if commanding his troops! Especially after seeking out information upon entry, and none was given. What's wrong with him!?

I believe respect

is the missing ingredient.

If you want respect, give it.

It is time to push back with a dose of his own medicine. Seething, I let him have it! **"LOOK, MR. RANGER! I WAS TOLD NOTHING ABOUT EQUESTRIAN RULES AT THE GATE AND THERE IS NOTHING ON THE MAP REGARDING TRAILER PARKING!"** I can feel blood sizzle in my veins as I blast him with both barrels, "I informed the gatekeeper this is my first time here. He told me nothing. This is a public park, with a horse stable! **Don't get nasty with US because The Dam Park doesn't know how to post rules!"**

"Go move your trailer!" the Ranger snaps back. "Park down the way on the dirt lot meant for trailers."

Would I telepathically know where that lot is? Shaking my head in disgust, we make an about-face and head in the direction of the trailer. The horses are tuckered out from running all morning. Inadvertently, we stumble back onto

Mr. Congeniality for yet another round of chastisement. We are just not fast enough for him.

We grow weary of dealing with his offensive behavior. I'm thinkin' the brig will be my fate if I don't rein it in and behave my bad-self. I dig deep, I mean, really deep, to find a tenor more pleasant than I used before.

"We are on our way."

Life is full of choices,

including the way we treat

and speak to one another.

The temptation to deck the nasty man or better yet, take the spurs to him, is barely overridden with common sense. Instead, a hiss and sneer for now. That is all the satisfaction I'll get.

Everyone leaves an impression.

I must ask of myself,

what is the impression I leave?

I ask the same of you.

What is the impression you leave?

I perceive we are getting the boot out of The Dam Park! Is this what is known as an escort service?

Tests take on various forms

to steal our joy,

or just make our lives miserable.

Sometimes tests disguise themselves as people!

Finally, the trailer is in sight. I look back at the stragglers. Sunny's behavior is bizarre. He acts as if he just wants to lie down. Mike struggles to keep him going.

"Hey, Mike, kick him in the belly! Don't let him get away with that!"

Obstinate does not surrender. The trailer is merely steps beyond the stables. What's wrong with this horse? The question looms. Why is he trying to lie down?

"Hang on, you can make it. Mike, kick him again! We are almost there."

The battle ends before the dismount. Sunny drops to his knees and gently rolls to his side! Mike quickly springs off a collapsing horse! Agility saves the man from being crushed and gnarled up in tack.

Faster than the speed of light, I jump off Cody. Yet Mike already performed his impressive Houdini trick.

"Are you OK?"

"Yeah, I'm fine." Blond curls escaped narrowly being crushed. "Is this normal?" obviously disturbed by the breathless horse lying at his feet.

I wish not to be an alarmist, but the adamant answer is, **"NOT AT ALL!"**

Sunny is sprawled out on the ground, panting hard, barely moving. Stunned and bewildered we watch.

I ask the spirit of revelation, "What should I to do?"

"Mike, let's get that saddle off him."

I loosen and remove the cinch from the ring, to slide the saddle out from under 1,100 pounds of dead weight. Yeah, right, what was I thinking? The gelding remains planted on the saddle, struggling for breath.

"I just want to die!" Sunny calmly tells me.

Did I really hear what I thought I heard?

Horses can be better

communicators than people.

Take a deep breath Reneé, remain calm, I mumble underneath my breath, "We've got to get him up," invoking everything I could think of to rouse this poor guy to his feet. This is serious. I don't want my friend to think he's done anything to cause this because he hasn't. We're totally untrained to solve this kind of dilemma. Helpless, we stand at the foot of a dying horse.

Did Sunny communicate to Mike the same message? Do horses broadcast their thoughts to everyone or just to those with ears to hear? I have no idea. I don't ask. I don't really want to know. What do you think?

Prayer is always my first option. The thought to call a vet never occurs to me. I wonder if Sunny will rise or die. After ten painful minutes, relief comes, Sunny rises!

"Come on, boy, let's go home!" I point his nose to the trailer gate, but Sunny won't go in. "Step up, Sunny!" Responsive as a statue, not the cooperative Quarter Horse I know.

"NO!" I cry out in distress, spin around in circles and stomp, "Of all places, NOT here!"

Adventures and tests

don't always announce their arrival

or

come packaged the way we want.

Sometimes they just slap you in the face

and say,

"Surprise, I'm here!"

It's a simple rule. I have no choice. If Sunny won't load, he must stay. We slowly trudge our way to the stable. With head hung low, Sunny follows. Soulful whickers flutter in the breeze.

I locate an empty stall some distance from the other horses to pen up Sunny. Then begin to search for signs of humanity.

"Hello, is anybody here?" I call out in hopes someone on the grounds will hear. "HELLO."

I hear no voices, so I poke my head inside the barn. There must be someone on the property! They rent horses, right? This has all the earmarks of privately owned stock. No ragged tack. Colorful headstalls hang over individual pens. Odd for a horse rental.

"Hello?"

The only reply heard is that of horses gnawing on hay and tails swatting flies. There! Tacked to the office door amongst the clutter, is a weathered curled torn piece of paper with a scribbled contact number. Anxious to explain my dilemma, I draw out my cell.

Ring ring ring; ringing turns into voice mail. Bummer! "You have reached The Park Riding Stables, offering hourly rides. We're not available right now, but if you'd leave a message after the tone..." the automated voice prompts.

"Hi, my name is Reneé, I have my horse here at your stable. For some reason he won't load in the trailer. I'm going to feed him some hay and we'll be back in the morning. I'll pay you. Sorry for any inconvenience. Here's the number to reach me."

What more can I do? The Dam Park closes at five.

I need the cavalry for this quandary. The only salvation to be found is my dad. I call him. "Daddy, can you help me in the morning? I might need assistance to load Sunny into the trailer."

"Sure, I don't know how I can help, but I'll go with you."

My relationship with my father over the years has never been great, although, as we get older, it has become less adversarial. Only a few times in my life have I ever asked him for help. This is one of those times.

Tomorrow's a new day; after a good night's rest, Sunny will recover and be back to his ol' self.

Tests reveal what we are made of!

We're not always what we think we are.

I think I failed this test!

Maybe I'll have opportunity for redemption!

~~~~~

Some might think I have been brutal in this chapter. The truth is not always pleasant. I wish I had never been given the material to write about. The truth is,

We often encounter mean people in this world.

Some live with them,

others work with them

and some share family ties.

Sometimes WE are them!

It's easy to point the finger at those mean people, but we all could stand to take a good hard look at the image in the mirror who accuses.

Am I like that?

Anger and Hostility

What drives us to this point?

Is all heart gone?

Has betrayal taken its place?

Do circumstances

Become our new dictator?

Is the voice of reason replaced

With anger and displeasure?

Filling our soul

Contaminating everything we touch?

Oh anger

How long must I hold on to thee?

Road Blocks

20

A nasty call rudely awakens me. "How dare you steal my hay! Come get your horse!" Click.

Agitated I speak into the dead phone line, "A lovely good morning to you as well!" There's nothing pleasant about being on the receiving end of a hostile call.

I pull my scruffy self out of bed, lace up my dusty boots and grab a bite. In the twilight of the morning this tired butt drags out the door to pick up my dad.

Daddy had a horse as a child. I thought his experience might come in handy to load Sunny. Not your normal wrangler type, Daddy is a 75-year-old man. After yesterday, who knows what I'll run into? If nothing else, he can bail me out of jail! Lord only knows, I just might need it.

Some days I flow in brilliance; it just happens. I can't help myself. Then there are the days I flow in stupidity. This is starting off as one of those days. I'm slightly confused by the stable entrance. There's a one-way sign on the narrow road pointing traffic the opposite direction I wish to go. It doesn't make any sense to me. An executive decision is made. Don't follow the sign; instead go the opposite way of the arrow. Shall we say, the more direct path. At seven in the morning, who cares anyway? Yesterday there were no signs; today they all point the wrong direction.

If the sign had said:

DANGER! WARNING! STAY OUT!

Would I have paid any attention to it?

Signs are posted for direction and protection.

As an added bonus, if we follow directions,

we save ourselves from the appearance

of sheer stupidity!

The stable is right there, I can see it. But who would have guessed?!! Headed directly towards me is a truck and trailer, bigger than life. Mercy! Now I have a real dilemma!

Here we are, stuck in a roadblock of my own doing. The only thing between Sunny and me is a self-induced traffic jam. Now, one might say, what's the big deal? Just drive off the side of the road. If it was that easy, I would. I would take your advice and go around the truck, which obstructs my path, but there is a drainage ditch on either side of the road. There's no way to go through or around without damaging my truck or trailer.

"Great, just great! Really? At seven a.m.?" I shake my head in disbelief. "Who would have thunk? Just my luck! How stupid can I get?"

Daddy quietly suggests, "You're going to have to back

up."

"Yeah, OOOO, man, it's tight!" I analyze the precarious situation glancing through the side and rear-view mirrors. "Reneé, you created this mess! Now figure it out."

Another reason to bring Daddy. My father owns several camping trailers. Certainly, his expertise will deliver me from this horrible quandary. With expectant collaboration, I ask, "Daddy, have you ever backed up a trailer on a narrow road?"

Snickering, either at me or my dilemma, he responds, "Nope! But you'll hone those trailering skills with this one."

See where assumptions will get ya?

Don't assume people know anything,

even if they should.

"Great..." I grumble. It doesn't hurt to ask. So much for drawing on someone's assumed experience. I struggle to back up. The trailer falls into the ditch not just once, but numerous times. The oncoming driver patiently waits for this foolish driver (me) who is going the wrong direction to get out of his way. If he is laughing or cussin' at me, I don't know. It gives him something to talk about. A silly babe being more stupid than he's ever been in his entire life, I am sure.

Sometimes we must dig ourselves

out of our own mess.

I try to get out of the way.

Back up.

Fall in the ditch.

Pull forward.

Get out of the ditch.

Back up.

Repeat.

You should try to maneuver the wheels of a locomotive and avoid ditches on either side of the road. It's hard, I tell ya! It might be different if a novice wasn't behind the wheel. Hear tell many RV drivers aren't any better at this task. Not that this is any excuse, only to say, I'm not the only one who struggles with trailer maneuver issues.

Finally, the thought occurs to me: I don't need to turn around, just slip off the road long enough to allow the truck to pass! So what, if I fall in the ditch? I've been in the ditch all morning! DUH! How simple is that? I guess if my dazzling brilliance was flowing, directions would have been followed, but no, stupidity reigns supreme.

If you waller in the ditch long enough

you'll either figure it out

or stay in and whine.

Just know if you choose to grumble,

it makes you look really bad!

Daddy doesn't chastise me, which I appreciate. My plate is full enough to resolve the issue at hand. A discussion of my incompetence and irrational thinking is nothing I need or, for that matter, want to hear.

What seemed to be a minor event

in the scope of life

became a pleasant memory of my father

whom I often perceived as being harsh.

Don't underestimate the impact of

simplicity or insignificance.

FINALLY, after twenty minutes of wrestling the ditch with a directionally challenged trailer (whose driver is no better), we arrive at the stable.

Don't allow roadblocks to deter

you from your goal.

Roadblocks take on different appearances.

People or circumstances,

for example.

They are not always as obvious

as a posted sign.

All my prior encounters with those in the equine world have been very pleasant. The common thread is real, down-to-earth, warm, friendly people for whom the animals' welfare is of foremost importance. This, however, is NOT one of those experiences. Now remember, the people at the stable have never met me. I am not looking for a hand-out, merely understanding. Or maybe a little compassion.

There's a whole lot of action happening in this parking lot. A small crowd hovers over a horse, possibly a vet or farrier. Flamin' red hair emerges as a vampire from the hub-bub. She's wearin' kick-ass boots with hostility in her gait. If fiery eyes could pierce a heart, I'd be dead. Nostrils flare in determination. She thirsts for blood! Barbaric Barb wields her sharp tongue as a sword in a vicious attack! **"How dare you subject my horses to disease! You had no business leaving your horse overnight. And the**

nerve to steal my hay!!"

I take great exception to her accusatory statement! **"Hold on there just one minute!"** I spout off, "I called numerous times yesterday. I had a horse who wouldn't load. Not diseased! I separated him from the herd and told you that I'd pay for hay! There is no call for your hostility! What if this was your horse?"

On the heels of yesterday's experience, I don't need this aggravation. Once again, I find myself subjected to the same brutal treatment. What is wrong with these Dam Park personnel? Why are they so hateful?

When everything seems to

come against you,

take a deep breath!

You'll get through it.

This is not the end!

I struggle to pull a five-dollar bill out of my pocket. Five dollars is more than enough to buy a bale of hay, even though I only used two flakes. Resentfully, I pry tight-fisted fingers open to post bail. Daddy retrieves Sunny. I planned to donate twenty dollars to the cause, but that was yesterday.

Perturbed, I mutter, under my breath, "May your day be as pleasant as you've made mine! Don't worry about your horses being diseased; the infectious virus you and the Park Ranger carry is far more dangerous! Nasty and hostile has already warped and twisted you, and you don't even see it." The park's personnel, not the horses, are in desperate need of vaccinations!

Highly motivated, we can't hustle fast enough to get out of here! Sunny obviously feels the same way. Without hesitation, he jumps right in. Daddy pulls the curb chain across his butt and shuts the trailer gate. Our business here is done!

Amazingly,
when you least expect life to go well,
it does!

I've dealt with a lot of women over the years, but none compare to Barbaric Barb. Nasty woman! I'd rather deal with an obstinate horse than a woman on the rampage any day of the week. Akin to steer wrestlin'!

We exit on the road we entered. I never look in the rearview mirror.

Oh, memories, how they last!

I'm not sure that today's test

results were any better than yesterdays.

Some tests are nearly impossible to pass.

Sunny, Reneé, and Cody

Goodbye

21

"**Doc, Sunny** wants to die."

"Horses don't just want to die," retorts Dr. Joo. (Pronounced Yo).

"I tell you, Doctor Joo, Sunny wants to die!"

"Son of a banana! I be there in hour." He too senses the urgency.

"Thank you so much, Doc, I really appreciate it. I'll see you soon."

As promised, an hour later the vet blazes up the drive in his old Jeep with toolbox in hand. Doc has practiced many years. In his mid-sixties, his tired frame struggles to move about with ease. Makes you wonder if retirement is near. Favoring his bum knee, he hobbles over to look at Sunny, puts the stethoscope to his ears, and listens to the horse's heart and lungs. Doctor Joo cringes. Softly, in his broken Hungarian English, he says, "Reneé, you right, you horse want die."

"I told you! I knew it!" Overcome with horrible sadness mixed with redemption.

"Reneé, he bad, you no ride him no more. Very dangerous, no ride. He lung collapse." He shakes his head in condolence. "Nothing I do for him. Very sorry."

"What should I do?" Bewildered, I question Dr. Joo. I have never dealt with such a thing. All I know is Sunny wants to die. Beyond that, I know nothing about etiquette for a dying horse.

"Two option, Reneé. Put Sunny down for fee. You call renderer, who haul away for fee. Or, you take to Fort Collins auction. They pay weight, dollar per pound."

Even though I know Sunny wants to die, I'm still shaken by the news. "This is tragic! I'll have to think about it. I don't know what to do. It's so sudden."

The Doctor leaves me with these words before he gimps back to his truck. "Difficult decision. Let me know, Reneé, want put Sunny down."

"Thank you, I will." Sadly, I wave goodbye.

Sunny and I remain alone...

    Heartbroken...tearful...hopeless.

    I snuggle into Sunny.

Lean against his chest.

Arms wrapped tightly around his neck.

My shoulder bears the weight of Sunny's

compassionate, gentle and affectionate hug.

Courageous and content, we embrace.

Giving and receiving comfort.

A good five, maybe ten minutes pass.

Sunny thanks me for such a great time we had.

I am overcome with emotion.

An encounter that blew me away

I never imagined

such emotion from a horse.

Such gratitude,

such love,

is overwhelming.

Sunny's special way of saying goodbye. Uncontrollably, I weep.

~~~~

Cash is not plentiful. The expense of putting Sunny down and having him hauled away is overwhelming. I agonize over the painful decision, yet, I don't want to traumatize Cody or us with witnessing such a difficult event, either.

Phone calls are made to the auction block. I want to know how Sunny will be treated and handled.

"Will he suffer?" I tearfully ask the compassionate lady on the other end of the phone. "I don't want him to suffer."

"It's very humane. We'll take good care of him; we continue to feed him up to the very end." The reassurance of her gentle voice on the other end echoes in my ear. I sense she understands my sorrow.

It takes us a week to make our painful decision.

Ben solemnly volunteers, "Sunshine and I will take Sunny to Fort Collins in the morning."

The auction starts at ten o'clock. A long two-hour drive plus load time awaits. I head to work with a heavy heart. It's eleven o'clock. I'm a little on edge while styling Leta's hair. She's familiar with the situation, but today's event has not been disclosed. Our conversation is interrupted with a startling telephone ring.

Enthusiastically Ben shares, "We got five hundred for him." The words amplify over a static-filled line. "It's really something to watch. He's running around the arena, crazy-like, working up a lather." It takes a lot to excite the man. This is the most passion he's expressed in years.

I hear Sunny nicker, painfully saying "*goodbye.*" It breaks my heart to hear him in distress.

"Oh, by the way, another thing happened, you won't believe it!"

What could be so unbelievable? "What happened?"

"After we unloaded Sunny from the trailer, the floor partially collapsed!"

"Oh, my Lord! You can't be serious?" I went hysterical.

"You mean to tell me, Sunny could have fallen through the floor on the highway?"

"Yeah, strange, huh?" Ben notes.

"I got to go, we'll talk later, goodbye."

"Bye."

In shock and dismay, I hang up the phone, unnerved by Sunny's whinny and near tragedy.

Not suspecting what just transpired, Leta asks, "How's Sunny?"

I can't even respond. Sobbing, I dash off to the bathroom, horribly upset. I had no idea it would impact me to this degree. I'm a mess, an absolute mess. I can't believe my reaction.

He's Cody's friend, I justify in my head.

I hardly ever rode him.

I've only had him for nine months.

The impact of a nine-month friendship

with a horse and a moving embrace.

Who would have imagined?

I had no idea.

JUST NO IDEA.

GOODBYE, SUNNY.

We will miss you.

Grief

Is the most unpleasant encounter

Never desired by anyone

Yet befalls us all

Amazing

The impact of a simple relationship

Not recognized

Until too late, if at all

Tell your loved ones

While they are here

Just how much they mean to you

And how much you care

RB

Buddy

22

Cody is grieving the loss of Sunny. But that's not all; she's mad at me for taking him away. After all, it is my fault. She has no one else to blame.

A few days following the loss of Sunny, I return to the barn. Rear haunches face me, but Cody's head is pointed my direction. Her eyes intently follow my every move. That is, until I enter the grieving ground. It's obvious Cody is disgruntled. Her attitude is cool as frostsicles. Poignantly she draws her head away, no longer does she follow or gaze at me.

Rather Cody snubs me, as if to say, *"Oh, it's you ~ the one who took away my friend. Don't bother me. I don't want to see or be near you. I don't even like you right now."*

"Cody, don't hate me. It's not my fault Sunny left. I'm so sorry, I miss him, too. I'll find you a new buddy, okay?"

It is futile to console her. She ignores any attempt.

People

don't always know how to react

to someone else's grief.

Do we ignore it?

Hope it will go away?

Do we talk about it?

If so, what do we say?

I say,

"Embrace the things you cannot change."

Share your condolences

with those you find dear.

Don't act as if their loss doesn't exist;

that only adds to their pain.

Hugs are good, too.

This cold shoulder routine continues for another two weeks. When I step into the corral to groom, she remains indifferent, ignoring my presence; she'll give me her rear end, but not her face. If that doesn't make a statement of where I stand, I don't know what does! My grieving mare remains in one place, staring out over the lonely, empty pasture. Grief is an odd fellow. I wonder if I'll find her buried in a puddle on which she stands.

We don't ride. I merely brush and pick. Oh, I might saddle her up and walk to the arena, but there is no thrill. It's a difficult time for both of us as we grieve the loss of our riding partner. I reassure her of my intent as I gently stroke her soft coat.

I've been reporting the ongoing saga to many of my salon clients. Today, I share the tragic demise of Sunny with my demure friend, Grace. She and I ride on occasion. She always rode Sunny.

Grace frequently travels to her folks who have traded city life for roosting out in the country. She has taken quite a fancy to the new lifestyle. Weekends are spent making connections in hopes of hooking up with someone special. You go, girl!

"Reneé, I know of a great, well-trained horse for sale. My parents want to buy him but aren't ready to purchase a horse yet. I've ridden him numerous times. He's a gem." Grace does her best to persuade.

"Let me think about it; that's a long way to go to fetch a buddy." I press Grace, "What's it take to get to La Junta? Five hours?"

"No, closer to four, that is if you don't stop. He's a great little horse." In her soft persuasive way, Grace justifies why I should buy the gelding. "They only want $1,200 for him."

"$1,200, huh?"

"Yep, $1,200."

In town, you can't find a good horse for $1,200. Maybe $2,000, but not $1,200.

"How little is he? I really want a good-sized horse, hefty enough to carry someone of size."

Grace continues to work me. "He's similar to the size of Cody; he's not very big. But Reneé, he'd make a nice buddy for your mare."

"I'll think about it, Grace." With that we moved on to other things.

~~~~

Time evaporates. Six weeks have passed, and I still haven't shopped for a horse. As soon as Grace enters the salon door, words take flight with exuberance. "Reneé, he's still for sale!" Relentless, Grace persists, "Come to La Junta and at least look at him. He's well-behaved, does anything you want and he's pretty too!" Grace is not taking "NO" for an answer.

How can I resist her gentle pressure? "OK, Grace, describe him?"

"He's light in color, kind of tan with a black mane and tail. Oh, and black stockings, too! I think he's ah-ah-ah-ah buckskin, yep, a buckskin, that's what he is," Grace recalls.

"And the breed? Grace, do you know what breed?"

"He's a type of Quarter Horse; they're not really sure what he is." Slightly confused, unsure of her information, she continues, "Yeah, they think he's a Quarter Horse."

"What's his background, Grace? Do you know?" With ignited curiosity, I begin to fire off questions. "How old is he?"

"Let me think about this a minute." She pauses, collecting her thoughts. "My parents' neighbor, Lloyd, told them that he trained this gelding when the horse was young. The gelding is now fourteen years old."

"What else can you tell me about him?"

"Lloyd sold him to a little girl who owned him for a number of years until she turned sixteen. The horse no longer holds her interest. Fast cars and boys are now more fascinating. Lloyd was asked to sell him on her behalf. That's all I know."

"Well then, Grace, I have no further questions, except when can I see him?"

Out of her purse, Grace whips out a slip of paper already prepared. "Here's Lloyd's phone number; give him a call. He's a really neat old guy." Enthusiastically Grace continues, "You'll like Lloyd. He's a real cowboy! With a ranch!"

"Grace, I'm sure he's great. Who wouldn't want to meet a real cowboy? And with a ranch to boot!" Tainted with a little sarcasm, I chuckle with amusement.

"No, I mean he's really a great old man. He's in his eighties and still tends cattle on the backside of his horse." Grace persists, "Reneé, it's a rare opportunity to meet a real cowboy!"

Teasingly, I pacify Grace, "Oh, a real cowboy! Who could resist meeting a **real cowboy**? I'll call him tomorrow and try to set something up for the weekend." On that positive note, we conclude our conversation on horses.

Later that week, I seek more information from my farrier, "Allen, tell me, how to acquire a decent horse?" I share what little I know of this horse in La Junta. Stooped over, shoeing Cody, Allen shares his knowledge.

"Don't buy a horse based on his size;

a well-mannered and well-trained

horse is a rare commodity.

Don't ignore that."

That is all it takes. I make the call to La Junta.

"Hello, Lloyd, my name is Reneé. Grace told me about your horse for sale. Is it possible to see him this weekend?"

Listening for a response on the other end of the line, I have no expectations; nonetheless, what I hear comes as a surprise. A strong, raspy voice questions another party.

"Edith, are we doing anything this weekend? This young lady wants to see the gelding for sale."

Chattering transpires in the background as they discuss scheduled events of the weekend.

"We are playin' our guitars down at the old folks' home at three o'clock on Sunday afternoon; other than that, we're free."

"How about midday Sunday?" I bid.

"Darlin', that'll be just fine." Lloyd follows up with directions to his home way out in the country. "Then turn onto the county road ~ watch out ~ we're not far from the old grocery store on your left." (That grocery store turned out to be a five hundred square foot dilapidated unmarked building.) "Then go two gates past the population sign. Turn right. Drive quarter mile farther, we're the rear house. We'll be watchin' for ya."

Lloyd is an experience over the phone. Forget the horse, I can tell, he alone will be worth the drive.

Hitching up the trailer, Deb and I shove off at daybreak for Colorado's southeast prairie. We follow the old man's great directions. Sure enough, four hours later, just as Grace promised, we arrive at Lloyd's and Edith's country home.

You can't be in a hurry; stepping out of the truck, we

know we just entered a different time zone. Country zone, I mean... l-a-i-d   b-a-c-k,   s-l-o-o-w, leave the city behind kind of zone.

Leisurely, we receive the grand tour of their quaint home, with all its additions over the years, including seasons and dates. Melt in your mouth homemade cookies and strong coffee are all part of country hospitality.

"Edith is an artist. We added on this sunny art studio for her to create." Lloyd lovingly sings the praises of his wife of over fifty years as he leads the way to the beautiful sun-filled room.

"Show them your work, Honey." Lloyd insists.

Paintings are everywhere. "WOW!" I thumb through some of her oils on the floor. "You're quite good, Edith. I'm very impressed!" (Which is not easy to do.) Turns out, Edith is a renowned artist, an unexpected bonus to our trip.

"You think that's something! You oughta see Lloyd. He's in a fancy Euro-PE-An magazine!" Edith proudly divulges as she leads us to the magazine rack in the family room. Edith pulls out this oversized European magazine. "Looky here." She thumbs the pages, knowing right where she's headed. Edith lands on a photograph of Lloyd in a brand spankin' new pair of western indigo blue jeans. Pressed seams and all!

"This group of fancy Euro-PE-An photographers with this American jean company came to La Junta, lookin' for some real cowboys with some age on them. These are their photos; Lloyd was one of their models. This happened a few years ago, when he was in his late seventies." Edith brags on her glowing husband.

"Great photos, Lloyd! Don't you look stellar!" Deb and I admire his natural relaxed cowboy pose.

Lloyd takes the focus off himself, "Now, this little gal we

know," as he flips through the pages in search of a different ad. "Ah, here it is. She too is from around these parts, a real cowgirl, she is."

The photograph captures a glow. Soft colors linger from the most gorgeous sunset over the Colorado mountains. This tiny waif of a gal shows us her curved backside. Her slim waistline graces a thick, lightly-sun-kissed braid. A well-worn hat is tipped by the cowgirl's right hand. Fingers straddle her left hip as an exclamation point! Now, that's a sassy stance!

"WOW! What a beautiful photograph!"

"R – e – a – l – l – y .... n - i - c - e." Gently I turn the page. "WHOA!" flies out of my mouth as my jaw drops! Totally caught off guard! The photograph on the turned page captures the frontal view of a sassy elderly woman. Deep pleats ripened with character fill her aged face. Her skin weathered and bronzed from years of harsh sunlight. The photo absolutely blows me away! What I had mistaken for sun-kissed hair is not. It is gray.

Growing old doesn't mean you need

to give up the things you love.

Lloyd glows with accomplishment, "It was really exciting to be a part of this."

Lips and brows lift with fascination, "I should say so."

Being chosen for such an exciting project at his age, what a privilege! This concludes our tour through this remarkable couple's home and life. Now for the anticipated reason for which we came.

"Do you care to see the gelding now?"

"Sure!" We certainly enjoyed this special moment of history; at the same time, we wondered about the horse!

"He's out here with Red. I got Red at Christmas, thus the name." We mosey to the exceptionally clean corral. "I saddled them both up so you could ride. Hop on, take him for a test drive, see what you think."

I ride Red at first, while Deb rides the little gelding. WOW! What an extraordinary horse Red is, a first-class specimen! Steady, sure-footed, tall, rides smooth as a Cadillac!

After the short test drive, I insist, "Lloyd, sell me Red," asserting my desire to have him!

"He's not for sale."

"Come on, Lloyd, sell me Red," I persist.

"He is a great horse, isn't he? I still use him on the ranch. Sorry, he's not for sale." Lloyd insists.

"You can't blame a girl for trying," with disappointment I accept his emphatic "No". I didn't bring enough money for this caliber of horse anyway.

Deb and I switch. She takes Red and I take the little gelding. We ride the sage-covered range imitating a couple of real seasoned cowgirls. Deb admires Red's qualities as much as I do.

We have all met people who silently walk in authority. They carry a presence. They need not say anything, yet you recognize it. That's Red. He knows his job and does it well, with authority. His gait is smooth and confident.

"What a great horse, huh, Deb?"

"He sure is a keeper. No wonder Lloyd refuses to sell him. Who could blame him? I'd keep him, too." She too covets Lloyd's exquisite four-legged animal.

"This yellow dun is a real sweet horse." I refocus my

thoughts towards the little guy under my saddle. Yeah, that one. The reason we're here, the buckskin. Just maybe he's a dark horse laying in the weeds, maybe. One could only hope.

The first thing I notice about this little gelding is, he walks straight through the brush, unlike Cody, who walks around everything! Another observation is he lags, never quite able to get those squatty legs up to speed. No match for Red's long stride.

"Deb, what do you think of the little guy?"

"He sure is little, all right. He's OK, I guess. He'll make a good buddy for Cody." After a long pause... Deb adds with as much enthusiasm as a wet fish, "He's not Sunny."

"No. No, he's not. Not in stamina or size. Nor is he the wise old soul Sunny was. However, he is a well-mannered and well-trained horse." I could tell Deb was not the least bit impressed. "Deb, I've been asking around, and for what I have to spend, it's hard to find a good horse of any size."

Deb nods her head in acknowledgment, giving me all the nonverbal cues of understanding, but remains decisive in her opinion.

"Have you noticed he has a hard time keeping up with Red? I believe he's smaller than Cody, if that's possible. He's a nice little guy, though."

Deb remains unwavering. "He's OK." After all, she and Sunny were great partners. Maybe it's grief talking.

Silently we head back to the corral. Lloyd has been pacing back and forth, anxiously awaiting our return.

"What do you think?"

"I think I want to take him home. He's no Red, but he'll make a great match for Cody."

Lloyd noticeably picks up the pace. "Let's load him up before Edith and I have to leave. We are singing and playing guitars at the nursing home in town at three o'clock this afternoon."

I guess we rode a mite bit too long for his schedule. We return to the kitchen table to finalize the transaction and have another cup of coffee and hear more stories.

Edith prods Lloyd, "We need to go now."

"We need to shove off, too." We push in our chairs at the table, exchange pleasantries and gather up our wares.

"Oh! I almost forgot to ask. Just one more thing Lloyd, what's the gelding's name?"

"Buddy."

Ralston Creek Trail

23

Hallelujah! Solo rides no more! It's a fresh new day to blaze life's trail.

Life is more enjoyable

when shared with a friend,

even for us independent types.

Three months have passed since Deb and I rode. I've missed our outings and Sunny.

"Deb, let's see what kind of buddy he is." As we saddle both horses.

This is Buddy's inaugural ride.

Buddy is not bothered in the least by traffic whizzing past. We slip into another world just under the trailhead bridge. A world filled with diversity. We meander along the creek's narrow pathway lined with cottonwoods in bud. Tender branches reach out and slap us silly while large limbs lie in wait to knock oblivious riders out of the saddle, if not careful.

Each time we ride the Ralston Creek trail; envious eyes covet everything about the parkway. Not to mention, the spectacular homes with unobstructed views that showcase snow-capped mountains. Yes, YES, **YES** I wish I lived here!

The woodsy trail intertwines with a paved footpath adored by walkers. Did I mention the golf course? They all merge together in this urban oasis. Tall-wild-grass shields frisky foxes. The creek divides golfers from wild galloping horses. For the most part, that is. What prime real estate! And to think we have the privilege to ride in this paradise. Are we blessed or what?

We gallop right up to the underpass... you know, the type cars drive directly overhead. The spooky underside looms low. Nostrils flare and Cody puts on a show with her infamous hip-hop routine accentuated by a dramatic snort. Nerves unravel. I want no reoccurrence of the "hi-ho, Silver" trick displayed on the streets of Leyden. If she rears up, the end has come. Not that I'm skittish or anything, but nothing can prevent the bridge's imminent descent. Time to bail before it's too late! Off the saddle I fly.

Buddy, on the other hand, does not disappoint. He is well taught, no sidestepping, no snorting, just laid back, and relaxed. What a hero. He behaves the same as on the open prairie. I could not have asked for more!

"Yee-haw!"

Up ahead, strange as it may sound, the horse trail merges with Westwood's golf course. Really, it does. We saunter through the crispy course. Despite the greens being golden-brown, it does not stop avid golfers. Scary sounds surround. Golf clubs swing off crunchy turf and balls whiz through the cool air. Cody's head and ears erratically jitter about in hopes to locate the source of the commotion. Laughter erupts. Cody can't get off the course fast enough! She's a great entertainer for all those watching!

"Chicken!"

This buckskin is fazed by nothing. No silly behavior, nothing. All in a day's work is his attitude. What an agreeable buckskin. Now it's time to see what this little guy has in his tank.

Deb and I exchange a quick glance, knowing the other's intentions. Spurs applied, we'll race through the narrow reeds and gallop around the bend, watch for pedestrians as we crossover the sidewalk, through the gulley, then sprint up the hill to claim victory at the ridge top! Only Buddy is in the dark. (We have done this routine a jillion times.)

A nod, a double click of the tongue, a good squeeze to the belly, a swift thrust to the ribs, and we're off! Charge! It's a race down the straightaway. Swallowed up by a narrow path of golden eight-foot reeds we all but disappear! Slap, slap! Supple reeds whip our charging bodies!

Buddy's in the lead... Cody rides his butt, I mean, right on top of his butt. Her nose rests smack dab on his saddle. Buddy's ears flatten, intolerant to the space invasion. Evidently, he does not care for a snotty snout on his butt.

The heated race continues...

Dust billows high above the stalks as crazy hooves fly.

The race emerges from the golden reeds. A quick glimpse

for pedestrians - hooves clatter over pavement before a dirt path is under hoof and downward we disappear into the ditch.

Horses are neck and neck.

"Move over, I'm coming through!" is Cody's attitude as she takes the lead.

We pass each other with a slight brush of stirrups.

Cody and I charge up the hill in record time!

Struggling to keep pace, the little gelding is left in the dust. Then I clearly hear Buddy say,

"W h a t ' s   t h e   h u r r y ?

I don't get it.

Why are we rushing?

Can't we just enjoy the moment?"

"Don't be a poor loser! Come on, Buddy, can't you keep up?" It appears Buddy has two gears, slow and slower.

Everyone travels through life at their own pace.

None of them are better than another,

just different.

Without ever breaking a sweat, Cody and I arrive at the ridgetop. Deb and Buddy drag behind, playing catchup.

"Hmm, so this is how it is? Really, Buddy? Like it or not, you're going to make sure we slow down a notch. I can see our style of adventure is about to change.

Bringing on a new personality
with a much slower pace

makes for an entirely different dynamic.

"OK, Buddy, we'll push you to pick up your pace a little and we'll relax a little. We'll make it work. We are in this for the long haul." I'm disappointed yet challenged by his inability to maintain the speed of adventure to which we have grown accustom. Although I'm not particularly happy about the slower pace, Buddy's stability and ease add a great new dynamic. I just need to readjust my thinking.

To be flexible to change life's tempo

now and then,

allows opportunity to view the world

through a different set of eyes.

I had no idea when I said, "we'd slow down a bit ..." what that would bring or how it would look.

Buddy and Reneé

RB

Mother's Day

24

Moms are meant to be showered with honor on this day. Call it self-indulgence if you like, but this year, these sisters choose to celebrate giving birth all by themselves, amongst wild horses and nature! We realize, this is not your typical Mother's Day fare. That's why we like it.

City dwellers exchange one type of wildlife for another in the heart of coveted Evergreen. What a splendor for the eyes. Giant pines whisper in the breeze, rolling hills house feasting deer. Wildflowers sing praises. Quaint and rustic equates to expensive. No wonder it's so desirable.

Planned suburbia is but a dim image in the truck's mirror. Welcome to Elk Meadows! Thrilled to be together, Denise and I chat up a storm as we saddle horses, paying no mind to the overhead brew. We haven't been riding long when white fluffy clouds give way to dingy dark ones.

Heavens announce their change in attitude with ominous claps of thunder and unwelcomed turbulent wind.

The rule of thumb is:

where there is thunder,

lightning is sure to follow!

I shout through the wind to my sis, "We've got to seek shelter!"

I recall a cover nearby. On the verge of hysteria, in search, we gallop from spot to spot. The mechanic's office is not what I recalled. This certainly won't work! Panicked eyes scan the hillside. Towering pines will do in a pinch. Hopefully the haunting thunderstorm will quickly pass. Instead, its showy friend arrives. Bolts of lightning terrify and illuminate the afternoon sky!

While trees are a lovely canopy

of protection from rain,

they are also a great magnet

for lightning strikes.

Trees are not your friend in an electrical storm, that is, unless you seek an electrifying experience. Intimidating flashes of light and brash roars of thunder have spoiled our Mother's Day party.

Spooked horses are difficult to handle. Horses' heads rise straight up; necks stiffen. Excitement and fear rule the tense equine dance. Unpredictable horses are daunting. The last place I care to be during a lightning storm is on the backside of an erratic horse! Shaken and vulnerable, sisters eyes lock, alarms go off. Fight or flight kicks in. Not just for horses either!

Denise bellows out, "Let's get out of here, NOW!"

Colorado girls know what can happen in a lightning storm, but not on the backsides of uncontrollable horses.

We bolt!

Painful bullets of rain assault us! There is no time to waste! Crazed horses burst from under the tree canopy with two wild women hanging on for dear life! Drenched horizontal curls head straight for the trailer! With a quick snap of reins, we abruptly avoid a nasty collision and bail from the chaotic frenzy!

"Denise!" I shout over the thunderous applause, "don't bother to remove the saddle. We'll ride in town when the weather breaks. Just get these guys loaded in the trailer!"

Buddy jumps in on the right side. "Cody, jump in!" Not to be left behind, she obliges with a quick hop.

It's terrifying to outrun a nasty storm on horseback. "We've got to get off this mountain!" Amid my own fight or flight, we jump into the one-ton dually. Heavy pedal to the metal, the truck tears out of the parking lot; rubber marks the path. Lucky for us, the stoplight is green. I put my foot into it and accelerate. Fast as legally possible we fly around the corner! Well, maybe faster. Okay, a whole lot faster. In our fury to escape this miserable storm an awareness of adrenaline permeates my being. Whatever possessed us to think that horses can't get wet? I guess the thought of being struck by lightning while handling excited horses creates panic. Whatever the reason, fight or flight took over. Fast just isn't fast enough!

Both people and animals experience

fight or flight.

It creates panic, fear and anxiety

which drives stupidity.

As we franticly turn the corner, we hear a loud **thud!** Truck and trailer rock.

Significantly we rock.

A deadly silence follows.

"What was that?" In unison we question with a shrug. Our ears are bent with anticipation of further movement. Typically, as horses reposition to find their balance the sound of shuffling is heard.

SILENCE...

We hear nothing... but silence.

"Let's ride at Van Bibber Park." I suggest with a huge exhale of relief. It's the park next to where Cody resided with her foal. "A calm lunch can be had, a nice reprieve from this morning's wild adventure, plus an outhouse!"

Drive time has baptized us with a hush. Adrenaline has subsided. Blood pressure and heart rate have returned to normal. "Reason" reappears. Wild women relieved to be freed from the grips of danger.

The truck's gearshift slides into park. Out of the cab we leap. Boots erratically crisscross the lawn to avoid contact with slimy goose poop blanketing the ground.

"Let's leave the horses in the trailer."

Decompression is needed for these two weary souls. Traumatized bodies perch themselves on the chilly, concrete table. The bench accommodates boots oozing in slimy green pooh. Cowgirl wannabes leisurely feast on sticky peanut butter and honey sandwiches recalling the day's crazy events.

"That was really frightening!" Denise shudders. "I was

scared out of my wits!" Animation amplified.

"Yes!" I concur, "The horses panicked, and so did I. Anything could have happened!"

Denise reconnects to the moment, "I could see us getting bucked off, fearful of being trampled underfoot. In all my life, I've never experienced such a horrifying event." she shakes in disbelief. "Let's not ever do that again, okay?" Chowing down, Denise recalls, "When the lightning began, I thought we were doomed. I sure wasn't after another experience of being struck!"

"Do tell! I didn't know you were ever struck. I've heard if it's happened once, your chances for a second increase significantly."

"As a kid in junior high, I stood inside the metal window well. You remember, don't you? I was helping Daddy scoop out the flood waters, during a lightning storm, when I was struck. It was crazy scary!"

"Wow, Denise. I had no idea. Zapped, huh?"

"Have you ever been struck?"

Licking oozing honey from my lips, "Never, although, I've heard stories. The son-in-law of a gal at work was struck twice, maybe three times."

"Really?" Denise questions the validity.

"Yes, really!" Sarcastically I respond before settling down. "He's never been the same, I'm told."

Still shaken from the ordeal, Denise expounds, "I hope to never repeat this experience. We may not be as fortunate next time."

We finish lunch and gather our trash. Sis leaps toward the trash can and I to the trailer to avoid green goo... as if we don't have any poop on our boots. Who do we think we're kiddin'?

Refreshed and excited, I ask, "Are you ready to ride? Let's go have some fun!"

Distracted by the absence of noise in the trailer, I give no attention to her response. My mind suddenly is preoccupied with the intense silence.

"They sure are quiet in there." Sauntering to the opposite side of the trailer from where we sat.

"OH, MY GOD!"

Eyes large as saucers, my airway collapses and my heart drops to my stomach.

"CODY IS MISSING!" My frantic shriek echoes through the park! **"Where is she?"**

I fling open the trailer door.

Blood is everywhere!

Strangers

25

"**GOD, HELP US**!" I cry, "We are in serious trouble!" Cody has slipped on the wet floor and is lying hamstrung beneath the divider, tangled up in Buddy's legs and a twisted saddle.

My head spins, we need to get to the barn NOW! Stan and Connie can help unravel this web. I slam the gate in a panic and jump in the truck in a race to the barn.

A car barrels from behind in hot pursuit. HONK! HONK! HONK! A woman hangs out the window and shouts, as she points to the trailer. "HEY! Your gate is open, and a hoof is dangling out!"

OH, MY GOD! I must not have latched the gate in the turmoil. Immediately, I pull the truck over. We jump out and dash to the rear. Cody's leg loosely dangles, bloody and scraped a bit, but thankfully not destroyed. Her eyes, the size of basketballs, glazed over. No doubt, Cody wonders if I'm trying to kill her.

"Denise, call 911!!" Shook up, I begin to pray.

"GOD, WE NEED HELP!" Faster than those words leap from my quivering lips, a vehicle stops.

"We can help!" a couple calls out as they jump from their vehicle, "We have horses."

God is faster than 911!

I'm overcome

with His provision and timing!

A tidal wave of emotion overwhelms me. My beloved mare's petrified eyes lock onto mine. I feel helpless. I have no clue what to do or...

Where to begin...

I didn't need to know...

The couple takes over. They discuss a plan of action. They work from the top. I stand out of the way and watch in shock, as the strategy unfolds.

"Loosen the saddle," the man instructs.

"Careful, careful," coaches his partner.

Gently, the man loosens then removes the cinch. Now Cody has room to breathe. Whoa, I deeply exhale, wiping my sleeve with drizzle. That gut-wrench feeling settles in my throat as blood pulses like a volcano from Cody's hock. Shock sets in.

The kind gentleman insists, "I need space to work, this divider must go." Rusty joints are jammed together from the impact. It takes ingenuity and brute strength, but the Good Samaritan frees the wall between the horses!

Thank God!

Cody calmly lies on the trailer floor. There is no kicking or struggling. I can't say the same for her owner.

The cautious couple gently removes the rusty divider. They make a great team.

If more of us could work together

smoothly in a crisis

the world would be a happier place.

Mission accomplished! She's not out of the woods yet. Words buzz about, yet I hear nothing, as the two consult one another as to their next step.

"Let's first remove the gelding, then unload the mare."

She echoes in agreement. "Just how, is my concern?"

"Hold on a second," I abruptly interrupt.

Horses are creatures of habit,

you know their response when

you've invested time in the relationship.

Buddy is no different. To gracefully unload is not a task he excels in. Buddy is in the habit of charging out of the trailer upon the opening of the gate, making it hazardous for anyone standing in his way.

That being said, my anxiety level is through the roof. I can barely breathe as a giant lump blocks my airway. My eyes cloud over. This heart of mine is ready to explode.

Before the trailer gate is open for Buddy to exit, I lay nervous hands on his hindquarters and speak peace over him and pray, "Lord, help him not to hurt Cody."

It had to be enough.

The rest is up to Buddy.

"OK, let him go," I tell the couple.

The gate is unlatched and swung open.

We watch...

All eyes are fixed on Buddy.

Oh, so s~l~o~o~o~o~w~l~y

An incredible

s~t~r~e~t~c~h

takes place.

Hypnotized...... time stands still...... and is irrelevant...... None of us can take our eyes off Buddy's hoof..... we watch the unimaginable.

It seems as if Buddy's entire load is on his right side. Ten inches lies between hoof and ground. Can a horse stretch that far? Will he collapse, bolt or trample her?

Breathe, Reneé, choose to trust. Five sets of glazed eyes are cautiously fixed on Buddy's every move. Gently, his left front hoof glides lightly over the entire length of Cody's traumatized body. On edge, split legs stretch beyond all possibility. The front hoof gracefully follows. Over her still body the hoof floats.

It's the most amazing,

compassionate demonstration of love

I have ever witnessed.

Equally amazing is Cody's calm reaction as she watches the agonizing process surrounding her.

Cody has a sense

to trust her Buddy not to inflict harm.

Hooves touch ground! I would not have believed it if I didn't see it with my own eyes. What an accomplishment! And without injury! We have success!

Yay! The lump in my throat dissipates; neck and shoulder tension melt away. What a sigh of relief!

In all probability, Buddy should have fallen on top of Cody. It's remarkable. I don't have years of experience to know or research what "normal" stretch capabilities are. Prayer is the only reasonable conclusion as to why Buddy didn't lose his balance. This outcome seems against all odds, but what do I know?

Never underestimate the power of prayer,

even if it's for your animals.

Cody lies still on the bloody, slippery wood floor, not wanting to move. Our eyes connect. Her dark, bulging eyes plead for my help.

I respond to Cody in the same manner.

Eyes are the window of the soul.

"It'll be OK. We'll get you out of there." It's a measly attempt to comfort, but an attempt nonetheless. Not certain who needs comfort the most, Cody or myself. Her hoof shows minor road rash. The hock on the other hand, continues to bleed profusely.

The emergency vet arrives as the Good Samaritans coax Cody to stand up. By her own power, Cody slowly pulls herself from the floor. The process seems rather anticlimactic after all the drama. A fountain of fireworks burst from these sockets of mine. The snotty sleeve mops up. Denise and I clutch the strangers tightly with a warm embrace. Sobs of relief are the best I can do right now. Words seem so limited and inappropriate.

Cody hobbles out of the trailer on three legs, as she favors the bloody left rear hock. "Oh, that's not so bad," says the vet as she evaluates the injury. "There's hardly any blood. Aye, she'll be fine. Stitches if you show her, otherwise she looks good. Just a little surface wound." On that note, she abruptly leaves.

WOW! Hardly any blood!? How can she say this? Blood is spewed all over the trailer floor! I shudder to think what a bloody mess looks like if this isn't it!

Words clash with today's bloody events. It all echoes loudly in my head.

"Just a little surface wound."

"She'll be fine."

We've all been traumatized, but she'll be fine.

A huge exhale of relief! Emotional hugs embrace the couple who sacrificed their busy day to help strangers with a horse in distress. These are not just any hugs. No. These hugs are filled with overwhelming gratefulness.

Thank you, whoever you are.

They disappear as quickly as they showed up. I never could have done it without them. I'm eternally grateful to this nameless couple.

God knows just what you need,

His timing is perfect.

Earlier,

Cody and Sunny saved a nameless lady.

Today is our turn

to be saved by nameless strangers.

RB

Choose Life

26

Cody gimps along. Our routine differs from the past. Daily I clean her wound while building tolerance to her nips of displeasure. Ointment to ward off infection is richly slathered over the wound before wrapping the hock in colorful gauze. Cody wears hot pink splendidly. Color makes us both feel better. Tomorrow, she will sport my favorite, neon green.

A need for a second opinion occurred to me. Instead, I dismissed it, after all, "It was only a surface wound. She'll be OK. There's no need for stitches." The haunting famous words recalled.

Cody's injury is the result of my stupidity. What was I thinking, carelessly speeding around the corner on two wheels? There is no doubt in my mind, the loud thud Denise and I heard was Cody crashing down, slipping under the divider wall. Why was I in such a hurry? Once they were loaded, we could have relaxed. What caused me to dart out of the parking lot, like a wild maniac? Insanity took over, I guess. I should have paid more attention to the weather conditions. My mind struggles under the weight of guilt.

"I am so sorry, Cody." She is in obvious pain as she drags her sore leg behind. This is awful to watch.

Four days after the injury, Cody's hock is just short of double its normal size, grossly swollen, and oozes with goo. She is unable to apply any weight. It dangles limp and useless. Protective of her swollen leg, Cody flinches to the touch anywhere near the injury. She withdraws from my reach.

"She needs a real doctor," I conclude.

I admire my Hungarian vet, but strain to understand his broken English. He's so far away and could be in the middle of surgery. Dr. Joo may not be able to respond immediately. It's imperative for me to know why she's not healing. This is neither routine shots nor exam. I've used Dr. Young on occasion, he's close by. My conflict comes to a screeching halt. The call is made.

Forty-five minutes later, in a whirlwind, Doc and his impressive rolling medical laboratory tear up the dusty drive. The midnight blue truck's shell is lined with pop-up doors. Doctor Young instantly pulls antibiotics, needles and whatever else from the shell's organized chaos.

He probes and contemplates. Concern is written all over his face. With a deep breath, Doctor Young explains, "She should have been seen immediately. It's **badly** infected; I'm not sure she'll make it."

I don't believe my ears. I'm dumbfounded. NOT MAKE IT? Cody has a strong will to live. Dying is not an option!

"We must try to save her, Doc! I can't just let her die."

"It was just a surface wound," no further action was suggested. My gut instinct was to have it looked at further; without excuse, I just didn't.

Don't ignore your instincts,

guts are more intuitive than brains!

I'd heard rumors about the vet who arrived at the scene of the accident. Her name was tossed around more than once at Westernaires. Unfortunately for her, it was always followed by a stern warning. I try to give people the benefit of doubt, not giving credence to hearsay. I just wasn't thinking clearly. Conclusions of what should have been done are easy after the fact.

When the brain is in shock,

it reacts so differently.

If humans need antibiotics to ward

off infection, then why not animals?

This greenhorn is granted an education about infection spreading statistics. "In a human, an infection takes days to multiply, but in horses, it multiplies and spreads in hours. We are already into several days. The results are grim," Doc imparts. **"We have to get her into surgery right away! It's imperative!"** Urgency expressed in words and tone. "I will make arrangements for her at the Centennial Valley Equine Hospital in Broomfield."

Unfortunately, I have salon appointments.

The Doc insists it cannot wait. In a panic, I call Ben. I'm not sure if he'll help, as our marriage is collapsing. But this is Cody's life we're talking about!

"Ben, I need you to load Cody into the trailer and get her to the hospital! Stan can help you." I rush off for work before Ben arrives at the stable.

Hours pass. Working behind the stylist chair, I answer a call. The exhausted voice on the other end declares, "She won't load."

My heart races with anxiety. "Eeeek! I'll be right there."

Hurried, I cancel my remaining appointments and find myself once again driving down the road in a panic. This is life-threatening! They should not still be at the barn. Surgery should be over. **Why have they waited until now to call me?** I'm boiling mad!

"That's enough, Reneé! Calm yourself down. You won't be any good hot-headed."

Up the dusty drive I roar only to see two sweaty men at their wits' end, scratch their heads out of frustration. Even Buddy can see, Cody is unable to get the weight off her hindquarters. It's her injury that hinders her ability to jump into the trailer. Ropes are under her buttocks and latched to the head harness, but all attempts to pull or boost Cody are fruitless. Nothing works. Absolutely nothing.

Cody has been fiercely independent and uncooperative before. However, this is not the case today. She's flat out physically incapable, crippled! All three are exasperated; it's painful to watch. I've seen enough.

"**STOP!**" I shake my head in disgust, "This is not working!"

Why continue to try the same thing

over and over again

and expect a different result?

I make the call. "Doc, we can't get Cody to load, we're still at the barn."

In disbelief, the voice on the other end cries out, "You can't be serious?"

"I know, the fellows just informed me a short time ago of their dilemma. What do I do?" My voice cracks under the weight in my heart.

"Do you have a trench for the tires to lower into? Or a place that is higher than the rest?"

"Yes!" I answer. "A cement slab, it's higher!"

"Back your trailer to it, she can walk right in without having to jump up. I'll be right over. She'll need another shot of antibiotics since it has been so long."

Brilliant! Now why didn't these guys think of that? This is no time for hostility or arguments. Just get that trailer against the slab. We do and breathe a huge sigh of relief, as Cody walks right in.

Dr. Young shows up just as Cody loads into the trailer. He gives her another shot and reiterates, "She may not make it."

She still has the will to live.

Will is a powerful commodity.

"I have to try to save her!" I hold back tears and slam the trailer gate. This equine ambulance has a half-hour drive to Broomfield. Fortunately for Cody, I'm not the one driving.

My heart beats as a drum in distress, fast and loud in my chest. I pray the entire way that she makes it, no matter what the doctor says.

We announce our arrival to the hospital staff, then hunt for a ditch to lower the trailer. With kid gloves we unload one hurtin' unit. Painfully, barely able to walk, Cody staggers to the door.

My body shakes from relief that my beautiful beloved mare is still upright!

The quiet calm demeanor of Doctor Judy and his assistant take the edge off. The two clothed in baby blue scrubs have patiently waited all day for us.

Painful stress does not inhibit this greenhorn's curiosity. Although I prayed all the way over, I also gave thought to how surgery is performed on a horse. Will Cody lie down before she's knocked out? Do they stand the horse against a table, strap it down, and rotate the table with some sort of hydraulic system? Well, I am about to find out. This ought to be fascinating.

We gimp through the huge hospital door and see a quite simple surgical apparatus. No hydraulics, no table; it looks like a cage minus the top. The doctor and his assistant scrub down, then insert their hands into sterile gloves. Like a drive-through carwash, French doors mark both the entrance and exit of this surgical horse snuggler. Cody is gently escorted through the contraption's rear door. Six padded panels surround her thighs to mid belly.

Doctor Judy calmly explains to Ben and me, "Cody will remain standing the entire time." He sits on his low swivel stool ready to begin the surgical procedure. The rear panel near Cody's left hock is removed; the doc glides his stool out of harm's way. Softly Dr. Judy instructs his assistant. "Give her a shot of anesthetic." Turning to us, the Doc kindly questions, "do you care to stay and watch?"

We nod with great anticipation to see how this is done. "Oh, yes, thank you."

"You can't smoke in here."

Ben removes his unlit cigarette from his mouth and together we step aside to quietly observe. We don't want to miss a thing or invade the doctor's space.

There is nothing worse than trying to do your job

with someone breathing directly

over your shoulder.

There is no sling to hold her head, only an opening to cradle her neck. The meds don't put Cody out, but certainly relax her enough that her head droops low. Cody nods off. No doubt sedation is a welcome change, particularly from the trauma of a six-hour load.

We watch skilled hands methodically go to work. He takes a syringe that resembles a giant needle. I hate large needles and cringe at the sight, briefly turning my head so not to see the initial entry. The doctor injects the needle into Cody's hock on the good side of her leg, flushing out the infection through the open wound. I watch intently the fluid and infection spew out the other side. He repeats the procedure numerous times entering from several different directions.

"Well, that's it for now," the doc states.

"That's it?" I'm surprised by the abrupt climax.

"Yes, we'll flush the infection twice a day for five days," Doctor Judy explains.

In an altered state, Cody gimps alongside the assistant and saunters down the concrete hallway to a recovery stall. A meticulous cubicle has been prepared next to another patient. Since horses are very social beings, companionship is bound to help the healing process.

You'd've thought we were at the Hilton. I expect to see the Budweiser Clydesdales in a stall next door. Everything is freshly maintained and of the highest quality and standards. This doctor does not skimp on anything! If he cares for the animals as much as he cares for his facility, Cody is in great hands. I have the utmost confidence in the care she will receive.

"I can't promise you anything. A long time has passed. She may not live through this. I give her only a twenty percent chance of survival. Come back in five days or anytime for a visit and see how she's doing."

My heart is pierced by Dr. Judy's devastating words. Wow! Twenty percent? I will not have it! Determination rises within my soul.

"In Jesus' name, Cody, **you will live and not die**! No matter what the doctors have spoken over you! **That is what I choose to believe and proclaim** on your behalf."

I will fight for your life through prayer.

Stand and believe,

no matter who says what!

God has taught me how to pray and believe for healing of my own injuries. It's time to practice on my beloved mare. I have no idea where this journey will take us, but I'm in for the long haul.

Every day after work, I travel to the hospital to see Cody's progress. The doctor's pleasant assistant is always surprised to see me. On the third day, she reveals why.

"Not many people visit their horses while they're hospitalized," she tells me sweetly. "It's really good for their recovery to have those visits."

I don't understand that; I love Cody. I want to come. To abandon her after such a traumatic event would just add insult to injury. I wouldn't want to be deserted. I choke back tears as her words tug on my heart strings. I refuse to intentionally inflict further pain. Cody has experienced enough traumas in her lifetime. If no one cares, why continue to fight? She needs to cling to hope. Hope to live, not merely exist.

On Cody's behalf I choose life!

The sweet young assistant expresses the doc's orders with certainty, "When she is discharged, Doctor Judy wants her to rest in an enclosed area, free of dirt, if possible. Confine her as well. Cody can lie down, but not move around or get excited. Is that clear?"

"Yes, thank you. I appreciate the time to prepare the barn for Cody's return." I will heed the instructions.

It's a very long wait... A five day wait... before the highly anticipated call comes. "She looks good." Pleasant words flow as spring water to quench this thirsty soul. "The doc says, 'You can take her home today.'"

"Yee-haw!" I'm in Broomfield as fast as you can spit to the wind!

Strict discharge orders overwhelm my head. "Keep her penned up in a clean, small area for at least a week. You know... she still may not make it." The doc clearly does not exude hope or optimism, at least not in our case. He fires off additional instructions. "Don't allow her to strain the injury. Cut up a diaper to use as a bandage. Always apply fresh antibiotic to the cleansed wound. Use only clean adhesive gauze and change it daily."

I cling to every word and acknowledge his directives, "OK

~ yes ~ I will do that."

"Remember, she still has only a twenty percent chance of survival."

"After all this?" I quietly question. I falsely assumed all this hoopla would increase her chances of survival. I guess not. That's OK, what do I care about percentages, anyway? I've taken Cody's healing to the highest power.

"Be prepared," Doctor Judy's strong words caution. "She's doing well today, but we've had horses leave and three days later they die in the pasture. The first three days are critical. Even if she survives three, she's not out of the woods. Five days is the turning point."

Wow! His stern warning injects pure shock into my veins. Stunned, we slowly hobble to the trailer. That cocky higher-power attitude is temporarily reduced to a holding pattern.

I reassure Cody with a whisper and rub of affirmation to her fuzzy ear, "We'll do everything he says. You will be fine, you will not die."

The timing is uncanny; while Cody fights for her life, my marriage deteriorates yet further. Cody is my refuge. Strange is the parallel of our paths.

~~~~

The weathered barn is a welcome sight. Other than feed, these horses find little interest in the rarely used barn. Yesterday I rearranged tons of hay, making way for Cody's refurbished accommodations. It's large enough for a horse to lie down, maybe six-foot square, no more. There is no indulgence of a cement floor at this barn. A simple bed of straw covers the dirt. Horses don't eat straw.

Buddy dances the quickstep as we drive up. Jubilation erupts as the two whinny endearingly at each other. It does all our hearts good. The trailer latch is unhooked. Cody cautiously steps out and instantly a curious snout zeros in on her wrapped hock.

Cody's head hangs so low, it nearly drags on the ground. Energy depleted; it's a slow go to the barn.

"Cody, this is your home for the time being," I tenderly whisper while stroking her soft neck. Apologetically, "This barn is not nearly as nice as your recent accommodations." Cody is filled in on what to expect over the next couple weeks or so. "Pretty thing, exercise is limited to short walks on a lead rope. No running loose, girl. Riding is out too, sorry. On the upside, it's a great day to be alive!"

Under normal circumstances, three times a week is customary to ride. Normal has a new look. Daily I drive to the barn, to clean, slather fresh antibiotic on the wound, change bandages, and check her healing progress. The count-down begins...

Survival of day one...

Warm hugs bathed in tears, fueled by tenacity proclaim, "You will live and not die."

Day two...

Cody's countenance drags. I can see her will to live diminish. No improvement is noted. Depression sets in.

Determined, I announce once again to my beloved mare, "Cody, you will live! You will not die! Do you hear me?" I firmly declare.

Day three...

No change. Tears cloud my eyes. Ache fills my heart. I'm moved by what I see and feel. Cody's life is slowly draining from her body.

"Cody, you will not die!" I shout as I wipe away tears of despair. "You shall not only live, but thrive and be totally restored, no matter what I see!" I sob softly in her ear, striving to believe my own words.

My friend Connie comes out and sees me lamenting. She senses the heaviness and looks straight into my tear-filled eyes. My friend speaks directly to my grief-stricken heart...

"Reneé, you have stood

believing God for healing before.

You will continue to do so this time as well.

Don't cave now!

Cowgirl up!"

She's right! We are only on day three. I can't cave now. Cody just experienced major surgery. I don't spring back in a couple of days after surgery; why would I presume Cody to be any different? This is a great opportunity to walk by faith, not by sight. Chin up, girl.

Keep your eyes on God

not on the situation,

as it will overwhelm you!

I need a good swift kick in the pants now and then! A reminder from a good friend to take my eyes off what I see, put them back on God, the Healer, the Creator, the Solution.

"Thanks, Connie. I needed that."

Day four...

Today the wound looks slightly better, although I see no

noticeable improvement in her spirit or will to live. I gently lay hands on her hock and speak healing and life over the injury.

The Doc's warning resonates loudly. "If Cody makes it beyond the third day, your mare is over the hump. It takes five days before she's out of the woods. Be prepared…"

Day five…

Breathe deeply, this is our day! I head to the barn for our daily routine. Honestly, with a slight reservation.

To stand in faith has great rewards,

even if it does quiver now and then!

She made it!

Thank you, Lord!

Dancing ecstatically through the barnyard!

She made it!

She lives!

Thank God, she lives.

Not everyone's hope for healing

Turns out like mine.

Some require more time

While others never make it to the finish line

Hearts are hard to heal

More difficult than bones

For their pain is rarely seen

Or understood, but God knows

He alone is the healer

Is my conclusion

For without Him

The pain is too great to bear

The journey of TRUST

Is just that

Nothing will compare

Time Heals

27

During Cody's recovery I, too, feel the pain of trauma. Divorce is ugly. The two life events silently intertwine with uncanny similarities. Lawyers don't give advice for the broken, but Vets do, so listen up!

Listen and follow the doc's advice. "Give her six weeks," he insists after Cody's exam. "She'll be good to go in six weeks. Don't let her run. Horses don't behave as dogs. They won't pick up their back leg to run. Instead, they drag it behind."

Those are the Doctor's orders.

Let rehab begin...

Our new routine consists of a gingerly walk around the

grounds. A great opportunity for a daily welfare check and a gentle nuzzle. For the most part, Buddy is mighty patient with the recovery process. Curious sniffs inquire as to our delay.

Some pain is more visible than others. It's a miracle she's alive and I'm not in prison.

The impact of trauma appears different.

Cody's spirit lifts as occasional deliverance from prison walls is granted. My heart is lighter too. All our spirits rally just to watch her daily improvement. As stamina improves, our walks lengthen. It's been two long weeks into recovery when Cody begins to act a little frisky. This is a good sign. I'm elated to see a notable increase in energy. This calls for some real good nuzzling, but it's not enough! Cody wants vindication. You ask, how can I tell? By her relentless tug on the rope.

"The doctor doesn't want you to run, Cody."

The next day I sense the same thing, amplified.

"Let me go, release me. Set me free!"

OK, I'm a big pushover. "I know I'm not supposed to, but my heart says yes!" No sooner is the rope released from her headstall than Cody picks up that hind leg, tucks it under her belly and bolts into the pasture on three legs as strong and confident as can be! Just as the doc declared would never happen!

What a sight! "You are an exceptional horse, Cody! Yes, you are!" Tears flow down my brightly lit face. Sheer joy erupts as my three-legged horse runs like the wind.

In living color, right before my very eyes, God's gift of healing magnificently displayed!

Another milestone...

Against all odds... Restoration cometh!

We extend daily walks to the horse arena down a short jaunt. Both horses come along. First, Buddy is released to play inside the corral. Sorrowfully, Cody is lead about on a rope. She grazes on wild alfalfa, ignoring the wild buckskin in the background kicking up his heels for attention.

Six weeks is upon us.

"You have done really well, Cody, I'm so pleased with your recovery. Let's ride and see how you do."

Cody is saddled and the three of us walk to the arena. I gently mount to see how she handles my weight. It's okay. Not bad, not great. I can tell she's still sore and shows great favoritism to her injury. After this trip is replicated several times, my instinct tells me, she's not ready to be ridden.

Trust your gut instincts.

Follow them.

Hard lesson learned.

Will she ever be back to normal? Will she just be another horse put out to pasture? Is she one of those pretty-to-look-at, but no-good-to-use types? Oh, what a painful thought! Breathe, Reneé, trust, before you hyperventilate.

Trust is powerful

It's time to suck it up! I tell myself with conviction and determination, "YES, COWGIRL UP! Cody will be fine."

I've learned my lesson. The vet is called. "Doctor Joo, I need you to look at Cody. It's been six weeks since her injury. I'm hesitant to ride her. Will you please check her out?"

"I come, one p.m." Dr. Joo warmly accommodates.

After a complete examination, Dr. Joo in his Old-World English tells me about his experiences in Hungary with injured racehorses. "I tell owners after serious injury, leave horse recover one year. She need time rebuild strength, be fit. She fine after one year. Some owners no listen me, horse ruin. Horse put down. Reneé, you no ride mare one year." He emphatically underscores. "I tell you, no ride for one year, you ruin her!"

EEEEK! "OK, OK, I will listen to you, point taken! I will heed your wisdom."

Doctors aren't always right.

For that matter no one is.

People just do their best

with the knowledge they have.

"Sorry girl, we're grounded again, bummer!" I'm terribly saddened by the news yet encouraged to know she will fully recover if I heed the Doc's advice.

Another new routine is established. This time, I saddle up Buddy and put a lead rope on Cody. Wrap her rope around Buddy's saddle horn with just enough slack to think Cody's the lead pony of this unorthodox arrangement. Joined at the hip, so to speak, not one without the other, we briskly forge ahead to conquer worlds unknown.

Jubilation erupts with each arrival at the empty corral! Cody's head tosses in the wind, her body contorts as a colt without a care. A rebirth of sorts, wow, renewed liberty, well, to some degree anyway.

Buddy and I ride close by. If we wander too far, we receive a stern reprimand, *"Return or else, I'll...I'll...I'll throw a fit! I'll hurt myself! I mean it! Come back. Don't leave me. I'll make noise!"* This is always the undertone of the constant whinny. It's effective, she gets her way. We've been spanked, so we ride close by.

Horses and people...

You know the routine by now,

They manipulate to get their own way.

Children train their parents

with threats or a whine to achieve what they want.

It's effective, too, because we cave!

The similarities are astonishing!

This useful tactic

is not limited to horses or children.

The repetition becomes very familiar over the course of a year. We don't alter the pattern much. Cody takes the lead on our right. Buddy and I follow close behind. The rope tightly wraps around the saddle horn to connect us all together. It's a handful all right, particularly in the beginning, but we learn to work together.

Soon we progress to the trails. Cody, Buddy and I have developed such a bond of trust and closeness. We know what to expect from one another, each taking his/her place in the trio. Cody thinks she's the lead dog, but she's not. Buddy just hangs back, relaxed, being a good sport, taking orders from his female commanders, just doing his job.

I'm often challenged for the position of top dog. Two against one! Not only do I have a 1,000-pound animal under my saddle, but another at my side. Who, by the way, has no bit or reins. Should a serious dilemma arise, we could be in trouble!

Great relationships require respect,

trust and time devoted.

It is only when those elements are met

that a great team emerges!

~~~~

Nearly a year has passed since Dr. Joo told me to stay off Cody. I haven't cheated, not once, I swear! The day longed for quickly approaches! Will she be a smooth ride? Can she withstand my weight? Can we close this chapter of our lives? I ponder these questions as the anniversary nears. It has been an exciting season for the three of us, but I miss riding with a partner. Months have been consumed with trauma, healing, recovery, bonding, faith building and growth all rolled into one extraordinary year!

On the front porch I stand, breathe a deep sigh of relief. The long wait is over. Today, the sun shines brighter, the sky bluer, the air scrumptious. A grateful prayer of thanksgiving is released before I leave the house.

All is still and undisturbed on this spectacular summer day. Hay sprinkled with grain is on the menu. Anticipation awaits completion of this morning's chow time.

Gently I caress and speak into Cody's ear, "This is your day. On this glorious morning, we will ride like old times!"

She is totally unimpressed with the significance of today's event. Nor does she heed my eloquent speech. Food has her total devotion. As if to say, *"You are annoying me,*

I'm busy with breakfast, in case you haven't noticed. Do you mind?"

"OK, I'll leave you be."

Stepping back, I lean against the split-rail fence and observe while they continue to enjoy the fresh hay. I wait and wait, and wait... "Just how long does breakfast take?" Smitten with impatience, I snap, "Will you ever finish?"

"FINALLY, you're done! Let's saddle up." I brush the clods off Cody's beautiful coat. "You don't want to look scruffy on your inaugural ride. Give me your hoof, girl." Hesitation to submit her left rear leg is apparent. The saddle blanket follows. Forty pounds of leather delicately swings over Cody's back before its tenderly lowered. I gently tighten the cinch around her girth, a little at a time, but not too tight. I'm not sure why I treat Cody as if she's broken, I just do.

"Suck it in girl," I tighten the cinch one last time. "We don't want to lose a saddle." I learned that lesson well! Etched holes indicate where the cinch once lived. Cody nips at my back. *"Check it again!"* A slight cinch readjust is much appreciated. "My, oh my, girl," I scold with a chuckle. "You have gained a few pounds!"

I test the saddle's readiness with a slight wiggle. I put one foot in the stirrup before smitten with a dose of reality. Oops, eyeing our compadre with a snicker, in my excitement, I forgot someone. "Hey Buddy, you wanna come? You'll have to pony alongside. Don't expect this to be our normal routine." Incessantly I babble like a toddler exploring its voice. Attention shifts back to the special one, "Cody, this is your day! It's been a long haul, but we've made it! Please don't stomp on my joy with goofy antics, ok? Are you ready?"

With lead ropes in hand, the three of us scramble down the drive. Take a deep breath, exhale. This feels like a first date. I'm nervous. My palms are drenched with anticipation.

At the arena's gate we huddle, hooves and feet all jostle for first place. Anticipation for the great "loosening" awaits the fling of the iron gate. Today, the honor to run free goes to Buddy. Confused by the sudden change in routine, Cody remains in my tight grip on the outside of the gate.

"What's this all about?"

"Hold on, girl, it'll be your turn soon."

Cody endures Buddy's enthusiastic dance, with head held straight up in the air. He's as stiff as they come.

I gently place the reins over Cody's impatient head, take a deep breath and grab the saddle horn. Insert a green and tan Ariat boot into the left stirrup and pull myself up. Carefully swing my right leg over her back before slipping my boot into the other stirrup. Softly my derriere settles into the leather seat. Silly as it seems, it is what it is. After all, I don't want to break her, again!

"It's your turn, Cody. Are you OK?" Concerned, I ask. She's not wobbling. This is a good sign. So far, so good. A few steps further. "How's it feel, girl?" Time for a slight squeeze. She doesn't miss a beat. Look at her gait, she shows no favor. NONE!

"Ya-hoo!"

Over the next several weeks, we gradually increase distance and activity.

"Today is your final test; let's open up and run like the wind!"

We leave Buddy behind in the arena. Cody and I take off in a full gallop, strong and powerful! I feel absolutely no gimp or favoritism in her leg. We never look back or slow down!

Triumph over tragedy!

"YEE-HAW!" Jailbreak! In a blaze we fly. Waves of tears stream down my cheeks. A sense of liberation floods my being! The long wait is over.

Victory, sweet victory!

My beautiful mare is not only alive, but plays, runs and can be ridden as before! I feel no difference in her stride.

Then in the quiet of the scared moment, it was as if God said, "Against all odds, she made it, you will too."

"Thank you, Lord, for restored health!"

Gratefulness marries elation!

I am overcome.

Oh, the sweetness of victory!

We can't feel another's pain

nor can we expedite their recovery time.

What we can do

is come patiently alongside

and support them through the process.

You know,

What you want done for you.

TV

The ol' golden rule

"Do unto others as you want done unto you,"

Is still worth its weight in gold today.

Happy Trails to You

May your heart be happy

As you travel on your path of life.

May the dust not be constantly in your face

Or the flies on your butt.

May the sun shine readily on your back

Keeping you warm

When the journey is hard.

May the lessons of life become precious pearls

To adorn your heart.

But most of all

May you find peace and laughter

As you embrace and ride the trails of your life.

EPILOGUE

Cody and Buddy remained friends for life. The adventures just kept coming. More exciting Cody stories are found within the pages of Renée's other book, "Priceless".

Skip lived out his life on the Indian Reservation. He received lots of attention in his later years being part of parades and ceremonial festivities.

Boot's horse Red, healed up from his bear attack. The flies coated the open wound, laying maggots. The maggots ate the dead flesh and the wound closed up. Thus, a great example of the purpose for those nasty flies! Red joyfully lived out his life on the Lazy Heart Ranch.

Cows no longer receive steroids on the Lazy Heart Ranch.

Grace found love, in small town USA. You go girl!

Daddy died in January 2004.

After 55 years of smoking, Ben finally submitted to the doctors' orders to quit. Nevertheless, a massive stroke took him in 2014.

Reneé happily remarried. Richard and Reneé call Colorado home. She continues to write and make the world a more attractive place, one head at a time.

Sunshine lives up to her name. Photography, painting and two beautiful children are her passion.

BOOK COVER

My daughter co-designed the jacket. Sunshine's graphic arts and photography expertise brought my vision into reality. Hats off to Miss Sunshine!

Monica, thank you for your touch to the newest Cody edition. Also, a shout out to Kaleb Persons, for your artistry.

Thank you Chaunté for the use of your horse, Nakoma, used for the front cover photo shoot! Nakoma was a gift to Chaunté and is now a gift to all those who catch her gaze.

NOTE FROM THE AUTHOR:

I never aspired to become an author. In fact, I struggled all my life with reading. One thing I do possess is great stories, which do not automatically translate into a great book. Writing didn't flow easily from my fingertips. With years of endless effort and tremendous joy, I offer up the third edition of "Cody".

Some names have been changed if they eluded me, in other cases, to protect the guilty from sheer embarrassment. Still others choose to remain anonymous.

My God dialogues are not fabricated. My job is not to convince you, merely share. God has different ways to speak, whether we listen or not. Sometimes we question or dismiss what we consider to be His voice, often rejecting it as ludicrous. We should seriously reconsider the dismissal.

Vulnerable are my thoughts, good, bad or indifferent. I trust you can relate. Our thoughts are not always true, they are merely personal considerations and not to be construed as anything else.

Self-employment has afforded me the privilege of pressing hard into God. This entrepreneur has no benefit package. If I don't work, I don't get paid. It's that simple. Under different circumstances, I may not have pressed into God. **Necessity births opportunity.**

This has been my personal journey. If you found "Cody Life Lessons" relatable, consider it a gift. Hidden treasures discovered are the most cherished.

NOTE FROM THE AUTHOR

Against all odds, I present my first book.

Nothing is impossible to those who believe!

Hope you had as much fun as I did. I'm fresh out of words for now.

Thanks,

Reneé Budde

Did you enjoy the authentic stories of **Cody**?

Read more incredible true stories by

Storyteller, Author and Poet,

Reneé Budde

Dive into her other book

packed with unimaginable God Encounters

Available direct:

authorreneebudde@gmail.com

Priceless

Dreams, Visions and Divine Interventions

Turn the page for a sample...

Priceless

Grab a cup of coffee,

Sit a spell….

I have a few stories to tell…

Lend me your ear

These are all true stories

I know you'll wanna hear

Of a lady on a mission

Not to be denied

Watch for the amazing

To open up inside…

God, Are You Real?

I recall being taught as a child, never question God or bother Him for the frivolous, bicycles in particular. Either I'm unteachable, rebellious or fiercely independent. Even as a child my brain just couldn't wrap around that concept of not questioning God. Why not? Is it forbidden? Will I enter the twilight zone? Will God spank me if I ask questions?

I'm now 20 years of age, raised in church, and never missed a Sunday. My hunger is not for more of church, but for a sense of knowing who God is. Determined not to be denied, I want to know, is He real? Questions mull about my head, probably not much different than your own. "God, if you are real, show yourself to me." Call it thoughts or prayer, whatever you want to label it; this is my question. Teetering on the brink of discovery, if God exists, does He play an active role in our life today or is he just sitting up there in the clouds discussing theology?

Several days later....

I'm driving down the street near my home in the middle of the day when an elderly disheveled gentleman on foot catches my attention. He acts confused. I slam on the brakes and leap from the vehicle. Is this man injured or lost? What's wrong with him?

"Sir, are you okay?"

He mumbles something in Spanish.

Great, I neither speak nor understand Spanish! Now what? I can't abandon the old guy. It isn't thirty seconds, when an angel arrives. This well-dressed statuesque gentleman exits his vehicle and walks over to us.

"What's going on?" The gentleman asks.

"This man seems to be aimlessly wandering the street. I don't know if he's hurt or lost. I have no idea what's wrong, he speaks Spanish and I don't."

Out of the front lapel pocket of the gentleman's jacket he pulls out a sheriff's badge, then speaks fluent Spanish to the old guy. Of course, I can't understand a word. Hand gestures draw attention to the matter creating the ruckus.

The sheriff turns to me and smiles, "He misplaced his belt buckle. He thought he might have lost it in the street."

"Oh, what a relief! Glad he's not hurt. Where does he live?" I ask because he didn't look familiar.

Interpretation reveals the elderly man resides at the nursing home up the street.

"I'll take care of him," the sheriff assures me.

On that note of resolution, I return to my vehicle and begin to drive away when I hear the Spirit of God say, *"See, I watch over my kids."*

CPSIA information can be obtained
at www.ICGtesting.com
Printed in the USA
LVHW041119240521
688317LV00005B/742

9 780984 663552